studysync

Reading & Writing Companion

British Literature

UNIT 2

studysync.com

Send all inquiries to:
BookheadEd Learning, LLC
610 Daniel Young Drive
Sonoma, CA 95476

ISBN 978-1-97-016222-6

5 6 LWI 28 27 26 25

B

Student Guide

Getting Started

Welcome to the StudySync Reading & Writing Companion! In this book, you will find a collection of readings based on the literary focus of the unit you are studying. As you work through the readings, you will be asked to answer questions and perform a variety of tasks designed to help you closely analyze and understand each text selection. Read on for an explanation of each section of this book.

Close Reading and Writing Routine

In each unit, you will read texts and text excerpts that are from or are in some way connected to a particular period of British literature. Each reading encourages a closer look through questions and a short writing assignment.

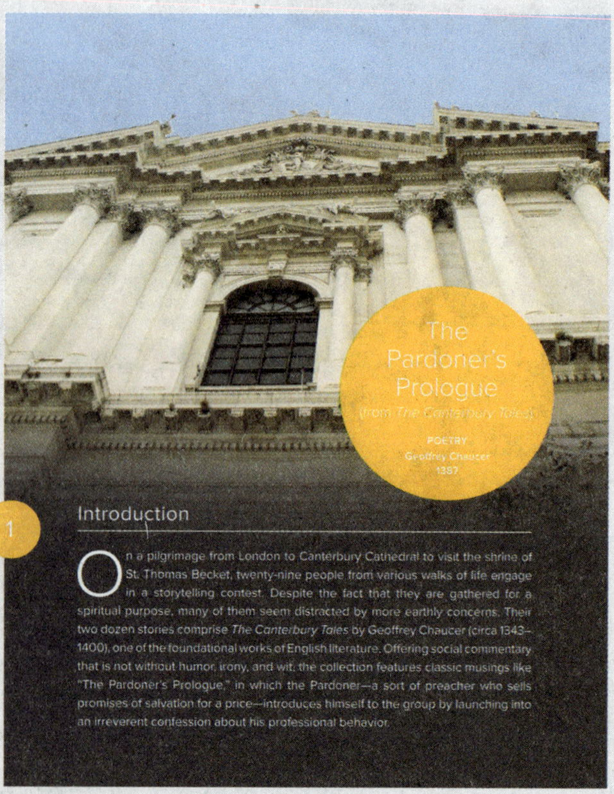

The Pardoner's Prologue (from *The Canterbury Tales*)

POETRY
Geoffrey Chaucer
1387

1 Introduction

On a pilgrimage from London to Canterbury Cathedral to visit the shrine of St. Thomas Becket, twenty-nine people from various walks of life engage in a storytelling contest. Despite the fact that they are gathered for a spiritual purpose, many of them seem distracted by more earthly concerns. Their two dozen stories comprise *The Canterbury Tales* by Geoffrey Chaucer (circa 1343–1400), one of the foundational works of English literature. Offering social commentary that is not without humor, irony, and wit, the collection features classic musings like "The Pardoner's Prologue," in which the Pardoner—a sort of preacher who sells promises of salvation for a price—introduces himself to the group by launching into an irreverent confession about his professional behavior.

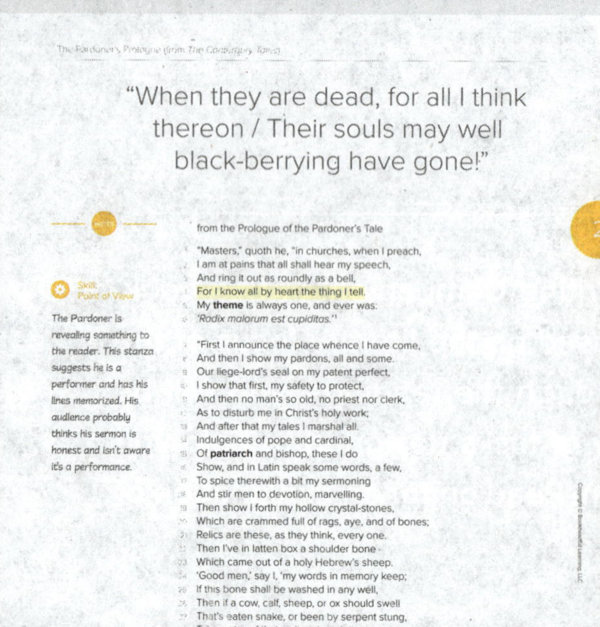

The Pardoner's Prologue (from *The Canterbury Tales*)

"When they are dead, for all I think thereon / Their souls may well black-berrying have gone!"

from the Prologue of the Pardoner's Tale

"Masters," quoth he, "in churches, when I preach,
I am at pains that all shall hear my speech,
And ring it out as roundly as a bell,
For I know all by heart the thing I tell.
My **theme** is always one, and ever was:
'Radix malorum est cupiditas.'"[1]

"First I announce the place whence I have come,
And then I show my pardons, all and some.
Our liege-lord's seal on my patent perfect,
I show that first, my safety to protect,
And then no man's so old, no priest nor clerk,
As to disturb me in Christ's holy work;
And after that my tales I marshal all.
Indulgences of pope and cardinal,
Of **patriarch** and bishop, these I do
Show, and in Latin speak some words, a few,
To spice therewith a bit my sermoning
And stir men to devotion, marvelling.
Then show I forth my hollow crystal-stones,
Which are crammed full of rags, aye, and of bones;
Relics are these, as they think, every one.
Then I've in latten box a shoulder bone
Which came out of a holy Hebrew's sheep.
'Good men,' say I, 'my words in memory keep;
If this bone shall be washed in any well,
Then if a cow, calf, sheep, or ox should swell
That's eaten snake, or been by serpent stung,
Take water of that well and wash its tongue,

Skill: Point of View

The Pardoner is revealing something to the reader. This stanza suggests he is a performer and has his lines memorized. His audience probably thinks his sermon is honest and isn't aware it's a performance.

2

1 Introduction

An Introduction to each text provides historical context for your reading as well as information about the author. You will also learn about the genre of the text and the year in which it was written.

2 Notes

Many times, while working through the activities after each text, you will be asked to **annotate** or **make annotations** about what you are reading. This means that you should highlight or underline words in the text and use the "Notes" column to make comments or jot down any questions you have. You may also want to note any unfamiliar vocabulary words here.

You will also see sample student annotations to go along with the Skill lesson for that text.

3 First Read

During your first reading of each selection, you should just try to get a general idea of the content and message of the reading. Don't worry if there are parts you don't understand or words that are unfamiliar to you. You'll have an opportunity later to dive deeper into the text.

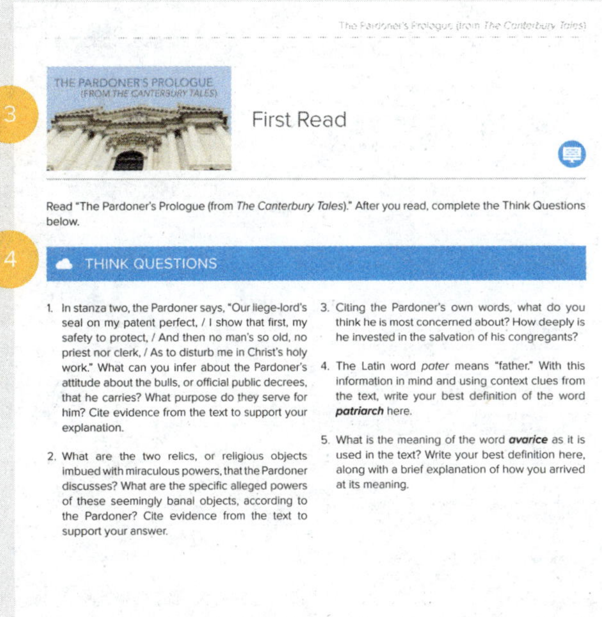
The Pardoner's Prologue (from *The Canterbury Tales*)

3 First Read

Read "The Pardoner's Prologue (from *The Canterbury Tales*)." After you read, complete the Think Questions below.

4 THINK QUESTIONS

1. In stanza two, the Pardoner says, "Our liege-lord's seal on my patent perfect, / I show that first, my safety to protect, / And then no man's so old, no priest nor clerk, / As to disturb me in Christ's holy work." What can you infer about the Pardoner's attitude about the bulls, or official public decrees, that he carries? What purpose do they serve for him? Cite evidence from the text to support your explanation.
2. What are the two relics, or religious objects imbued with miraculous powers, that the Pardoner discusses? What are the specific alleged powers of these seemingly banal objects, according to the Pardoner? Cite evidence from the text to support your answer.
3. Citing the Pardoner's own words, what do you think he is most concerned about? How deeply is he invested in the salvation of his congregants?
4. The Latin word *pater* means "father." With this information in mind and using context clues from the text, write your best definition of the word ***patriarch*** here.
5. What is the meaning of the word ***avarice*** as it is used in the text? Write your best definition here, along with a brief explanation of how you arrived at its meaning.

4 Think Questions

These questions will ask you to start thinking critically about the text, asking specific questions about its purpose, and making connections to your prior knowledge and reading experiences. To answer these questions, you should go back to the text and draw upon specific evidence to support your responses. You will also begin to explore some of the more challenging vocabulary words in the selection.

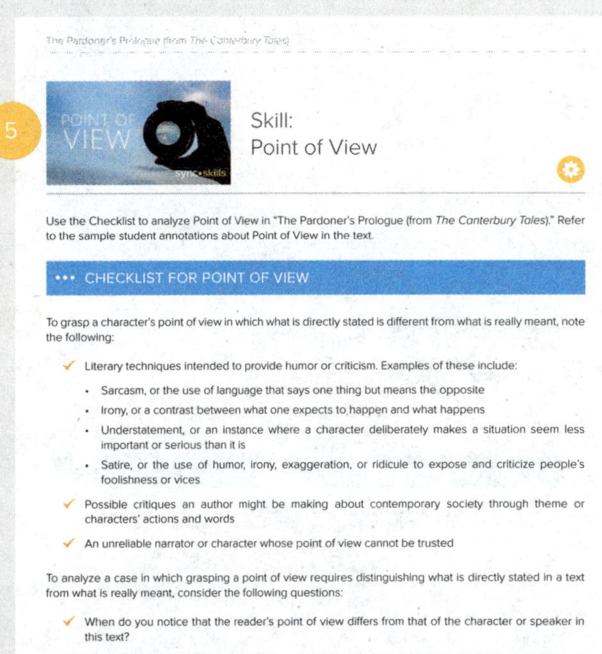
The Pardoner's Prologue (from *The Canterbury Tales*)

5 Skill: Point of View

Use the Checklist to analyze Point of View in "The Pardoner's Prologue (from *The Canterbury Tales*)." Refer to the sample student annotations about Point of View in the text.

CHECKLIST FOR POINT OF VIEW

To grasp a character's point of view in which what is directly stated is different from what is really meant, note the following:

- ✓ Literary techniques intended to provide humor or criticism. Examples of these include:
  - Sarcasm, or the use of language that says one thing but means the opposite
  - Irony, or a contrast between what one expects to happen and what happens
  - Understatement, or an instance where a character deliberately makes a situation seem less important or serious than it is
  - Satire, or the use of humor, irony, exaggeration, or ridicule to expose and criticize people's foolishness or vices
- ✓ Possible critiques an author might be making about contemporary society through theme or characters' actions and words
- ✓ An unreliable narrator or character whose point of view cannot be trusted

To analyze a case in which grasping a point of view requires distinguishing what is directly stated in a text from what is really meant, consider the following questions:

- ✓ When do you notice that the reader's point of view differs from that of the character or speaker in this text?
- ✓ How does a character's or narrator's point of view contribute to a nonliteral understanding of

5 Skills

Each Skill includes two parts: Checklist and Your Turn. In the Checklist, you will learn the process for analyzing the text. The model student annotations in the text provide examples of how you might make your own notes following the instructions in the Checklist. In the Your Turn, you will use those same instructions to practice the skill.

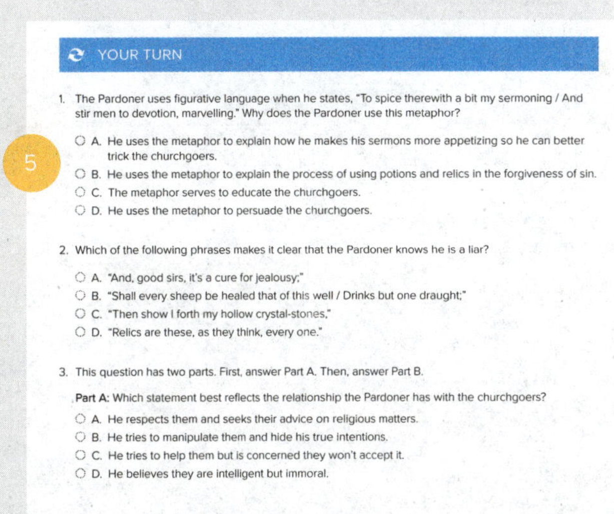
YOUR TURN

5

1. The Pardoner uses figurative language when he states, "To spice therewith a bit my sermoning / And stir men to devotion, marvelling." Why does the Pardoner use this metaphor?
   - A. He uses the metaphor to explain how he makes his sermons more appetizing so he can better trick the churchgoers.
   - B. He uses the metaphor to explain the process of using potions and relics in the forgiveness of sin.
   - C. The metaphor serves to educate the churchgoers.
   - D. He uses the metaphor to persuade the churchgoers.
2. Which of the following phrases makes it clear that the Pardoner knows he is a liar?
   - A. "And, good sirs, it's a cure for jealousy;"
   - B. "Shall every sheep be healed that of this well / Drinks but one draught;"
   - C. "Then show I forth my hollow crystal-stones,"
   - D. "Relics are these, as they think, every one."
3. This question has two parts. First, answer Part A. Then, answer Part B.

   Part A: Which statement best reflects the relationship the Pardoner has with the churchgoers?
   - A. He respects them and seeks their advice on religious matters.
   - B. He tries to manipulate them and hide his true intentions.
   - C. He tries to help them but is concerned they won't accept it.
   - D. He believes they are intelligent but immoral.

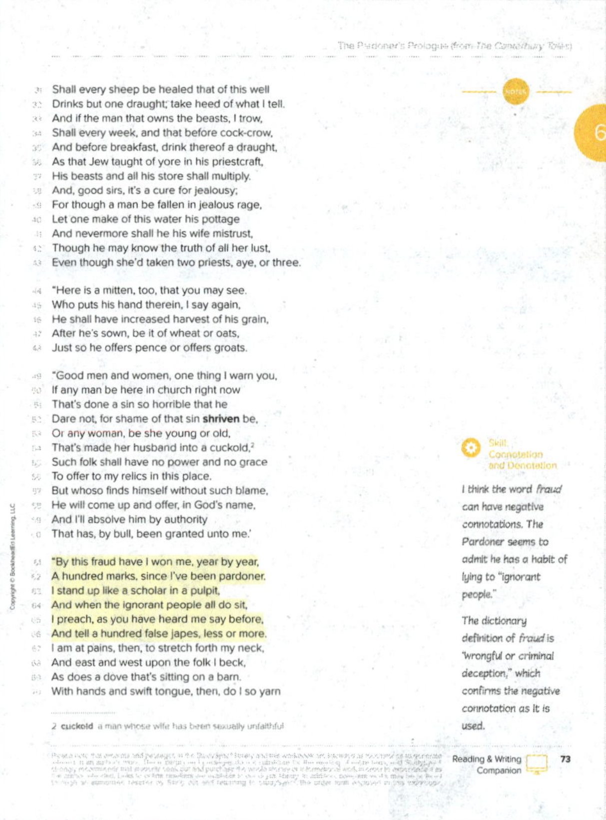
The Pardoner's Prologue (from *The Canterbury Tales*)

Shall every sheep be healed that of this well
Drinks but one draught; take heed of what I tell.
And if the man that owns the beasts, I trow,
Shall every week, and that before cock-crow,
And before breakfast, drink thereof a draught,
As that Jew taught of yore in his priestcraft,
His beasts and all his store shall multiply.
And, good sirs, it's a cure for jealousy;
For though a man be fallen in jealous rage,
Let one make of this water his pottage
And nevermore shall he his wife mistrust,
Though he may know the truth of all her lust,
Even though she'd taken two priests, aye, or three.

"Here is a mitten, too, that you may see.
Who puts his hand therein, I say again,
He shall have increased harvest of his grain,
After he's sown, be it of wheat or oats,
Just so he offers pence or offers groats.

"Good men and women, one thing I warn you,
If any man be here in church right now
That's done a sin so horrible that he
Dare not, for shame of that sin **shriven** be,
Or any woman, be she young or old,
That's made her husband into a cuckold,[2]
Such folk shall have no power and no grace
To offer to my relics in this place.
But whoso finds himself without such blame,
He will come up and offer, in God's name,
And I'll absolve him by authority
That has, by bull, been granted unto me.'

"By this fraud have I won me, year by year,
A hundred marks, since I've been pardoner.
I stand up like a scholar in a pulpit,
And when the ignorant people all do sit,
I preach, as you have heard me say before,
And tell a hundred false japes, less or more.
I am at pains, then, to stretch forth my neck,
And east and west upon the folk I beck,
As does a dove that's sitting on a barn.
With hands and swift tongue, then, do I so yarn

Skill: Connotation and Denotation

I think the word fraud can have negative connotations. The Pardoner seems to admit he has a habit of lying to "ignorant people."

The dictionary definition of fraud is "wrongful or criminal deception," which confirms the negative connotation as it is used.

2 **cuckold** a man whose wife has been sexually unfaithful

Reading & Writing Companion 73

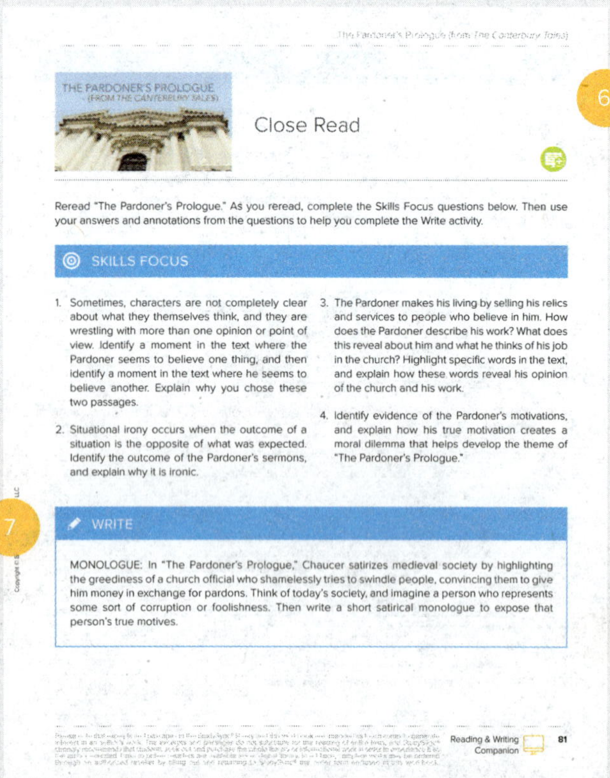
The Pardoner's Prologue (from *The Canterbury Tales*)

THE PARDONER'S PROLOGUE (FROM THE CANTERBURY TALES)

Close Read

Reread "The Pardoner's Prologue." As you reread, complete the Skills Focus questions below. Then use your answers and annotations from the questions to help you complete the Write activity.

SKILLS FOCUS

1. Sometimes, characters are not completely clear about what they themselves think, and they are wrestling with more than one opinion or point of view. Identify a moment in the text where the Pardoner seems to believe one thing, and then identify a moment in the text where he seems to believe another. Explain why you chose these two passages.
2. Situational irony occurs when the outcome of a situation is the opposite of what was expected. Identify the outcome of the Pardoner's sermons, and explain why it is ironic.
3. The Pardoner makes his living by selling his relics and services to people who believe in him. How does the Pardoner describe his work? What does this reveal about him and what he thinks of his job in the church? Highlight specific words in the text, and explain how these words reveal his opinion of the church and his work.
4. Identify evidence of the Pardoner's motivations, and explain how his true motivation creates a moral dilemma that helps develop the theme of "The Pardoner's Prologue."

WRITE

MONOLOGUE: In "The Pardoner's Prologue," Chaucer satirizes medieval society by highlighting the greediness of a church official who shamelessly tries to swindle people, convincing them to give him money in exchange for pardons. Think of today's society, and imagine a person who represents some sort of corruption or foolishness. Then write a short satirical monologue to expose that person's true motives.

Reading & Writing Companion 81

6 Close Read & Skills Focus

After you have completed the First Read, you will be asked to go back and read the text more closely and critically. Before you begin your Close Read, you should read through the Skills Focus to get an idea of the concepts you will want to focus on during your second reading. You should work through the Skills Focus by making annotations, highlighting important concepts, and writing notes or questions in the "Notes" column. Depending on instructions from your teacher, you may need to respond online or use a separate piece of paper to start expanding on your thoughts and ideas.

7 Write

Your study of each selection will end with a writing assignment. For this assignment, you should use your notes, annotations, personal ideas, and answers to both the Think and the Skills Focus questions. Be sure to read the prompt carefully and address each part of it in your writing.

Extended Writing Project and Grammar

This is your opportunity to use genre characteristics and craft to compose meaningful, longer written works exploring the theme of each unit. You will draw information from your readings, research, and own life experiences to complete the assignment.

1 Writing Project

After you have read all of the unit text selections, you will move on to a writing project. Each project will guide you through the process of writing your essay. Student models will provide guidance and help you organize your thoughts. One unit ends with an **Extended Oral Project,** which will give you an opportunity to develop your oral language and communication skills.

2 Writing Process Steps

There are four steps in the writing process: Plan, Draft, Revise, and Edit and Publish. During each step, you will form and shape your writing project, and each lesson's peer review will give you the chance to receive feedback from your peers and teacher.

3 Writing Skills

Each Skill lesson focuses on a specific strategy or technique that you will use during your writing project. Each lesson presents a process for applying the skill to your own work and gives you the opportunity to practice it to improve your writing.

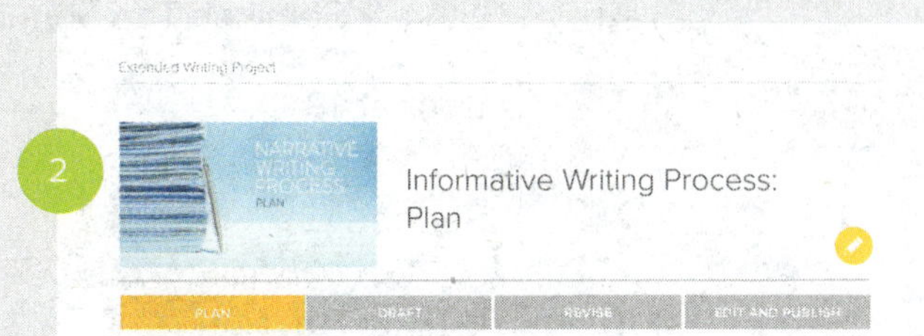

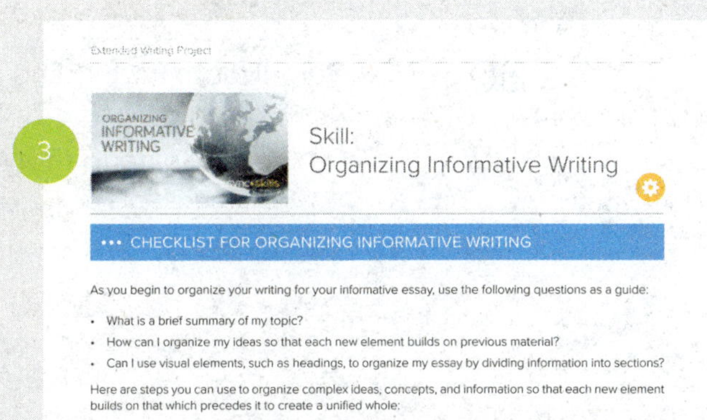

The Human Condition

How do we express the complexities of being human?

Literary Focus: THE ENGLISH RENAISSANCE

Texts

PAIRED READINGS

Extended Writing Project and Grammar

Talk Back Text

Talk Back Texts are works from a later period that engage with the themes and tropes of the unit's literary focus. Demonstrating that literature is always in conversation, these texts provide dynamic new perspectives to complement the unit's more traditional chronology.

Unit 2: The Human Condition

How do we express the complexities of being human?

BILL BRYSON

Born in Iowa, Bill Bryson (b. 1951) has lived in Britain since the 1970s, when he decided to move there following a four-month backpacking trip through Europe. A trained journalist, he has written a number of popular nonfiction books on subjects ranging from travel to science to language. His 2007 biography of William Shakespeare investigates some of the controversies surrounding the playwright and poet, such as the well-rehearsed authorship debate.

JOHN DONNE

English clergyman John Donne (1572–1631) was born into a Catholic family at a time of fervent religious persecution, which cost the lives of his uncle and younger brother. The foremost poet of the metaphysical movement, his work is known for using paradoxical images and conceits to explore faith, love, and death. In 1623, Donne incorrectly believed himself to be dying from the plague, resulting in some of his most well-known lines, "No man is an island, entire of himself; . . . therefore never send to know for whom the bell tolls; it tolls for thee."

T. S. ELIOT

One of the most highly regarded poets of his time, T. S. Eliot (1888–1965) was also a playwright and an influential literary critic. In his 1919 essay on Shakespeare's *Hamlet*, he put forward his concept of the "objective correlative"—a set of objects, a situation, or a chain of events that evokes a certain emotion in an audience. When asked about the difference between plays and poems, Eliot said, "There is all the difference in the world between writing a play for an audience and writing a poem, in which you're writing primarily for yourself."

QUEEN ELIZABETH I

For one of the most famous rulers of all time, England's Queen Elizabeth I (1533–1603) had a tumultuous early life. Her father, King Henry VIII, was dismayed at her birth—having hoped for a son—and ordered the beheading of her mother when Elizabeth was just two years old. After a period of imprisonment, Elizabeth rose to the English throne at the age of twenty-five. Her forty-five-year reign is considered a golden age in English history, during which the arts flourished and England emerged as a world power, defeating the famed Spanish Armada.

RICHARD LOVELACE

Born into a distinguished military and legal family, Richard Lovelace (1618–1657) was an English poet embroiled in the political affairs of seventeenth-century England. He was counted among the Cavalier poets, a group of writers who supported King Charles I during the English Civil War by fighting and writing on behalf of the King and his ideals. His time spent engaged in military campaigns and political imprisonment critically informed his most famous works, "To Lucasta, Going to the Wars" and "To Althea, from Prison."

WILLIAM SHAKESPEARE

Widely regarded as one of the greatest writers in the English language, William Shakespeare (ca. 1564–1616) wrote plays and poems that form the bedrock of the English literary tradition. When it comes to his personal history, however, very little is known. Born in Stratford-upon-Avon, England, Shakespeare rose to prominence in the London theatre scene, where he was both a playwright and actor. He wrote at least thirty-seven plays, many of which—including *Hamlet*—have become some of the most loved and most referenced works of any author in history.

TOM STOPPARD

Born Tomás Straüssler in modern-day Czech Republic, Tom Stoppard (b. 1937) is a British playwright and screenwriter. Stoppard's writing career began as a teenager when he left school to work as a journalist. A prolific writer who has also written a novel, Stoppard creates works characterized by their playful use of language and inclusion of philosophical ideas, such as chaos theory, consciousness, and free will.

LITERARY FOCUS: The English Renaissance

Introduction

This introduction to English Renaissance literature provides readers with the historical and cultural context of the period. The Renaissance movement, inspired by the reign of Queen Elizabeth I and humanist ideals, gave rise to one of the most prolific writers in the English language: William Shakespeare. It was a time in which human experience had more value than ever before. Independent thought, along with scientific and artistic endeavors, were more and more common, contributing to an inspiring culture in which Shakespeare could craft his legendary dramas. Meaning "rebirth" in French, the Renaissance gave birth to some of the most memorable and influential works in the English canon.

"To the humanists, human endeavor had dignity and worth in its own right."

NOTES

1 In May 2018, Nielsen reported that 29.2 million Americans watched the wedding of Prince Henry and Meghan Markle. Seven years earlier, 22.8 million Americans tuned in to watch Harry's older brother, William, marry Kate Middleton. Why are so many Americans still interested in the royal family nearly two hundred fifty years after the United States broke free from British control? The British royals remain international tastemakers. People from all around the world try to emulate their style and preferences. That remains as true today as it was during the seventeenth century, when the tastes of royals like Queen Elizabeth I helped artistic movements gain fans both at home and abroad.

Tudor England

2 The **Tudors** reigned between the fifteenth and seventeenth centuries in England. The first **monarch** of the Tudor dynasty, Henry VII, came into power in 1485. Henry earned the English crown after defeating Richard III, ending the thirty-year civil war known as the War of the Roses. His son, Henry VIII, ruled following Henry VII's death in 1509. Three of Henry VIII's children sat on the English throne between 1547 and 1603. Edward VI immediately succeeded his father. After Edward died of tuberculosis, Mary I ruled for a mere five years before her own death. Mary's rule was brief but intense. She received the nickname "Bloody Mary" due to her persecution of Protestants in an attempt to restore Catholicism as the state religion. Elizabeth I reversed this position when she took control of the country in 1558. Despite the religious and political conflicts that divided the Tudors, by the time Elizabeth took the crown, a burst of creative energy brought a golden age of culture to England.

Queen Elizabeth

3 Many people celebrated Elizabeth I's ascension to the throne, which restored peace after Mary I's short, turbulent reign. During her reign, Elizabeth was praised for her wit, eloquence, and intellect. Unlike other girls and young women of the time, Elizabeth received a strong formal education. As a result, she was well-versed in many subjects, including mathematics, history, geography, and astronomy, and literate in Greek, Latin, and several other modern languages.

NOTES

4 Elizabeth's reign was long and eventful. During her forty-five years on the throne, she overcame numerous challenges that came from religious conflicts, political intrigue, and threats of war. Many believed that a queen could not rule successfully without a king by her side, but Elizabeth never married. Instead, she proved herself to be more than capable of facing international crises and defending her country. Under Elizabeth's guidance, England became a great sea power capable of defeating its enemies, including the powerful Spanish **Armada** sent by Philip II in an attempt to seize control of England. Additionally, Elizabeth supported a flourishing period of cultural achievement that came to be known as the English **Renaissance.**

Painting of the Spanish Armada in the collection of the National Maritime Museum, Greenwich, England

The Renaissance

5 Spanning the fourteenth through the seventeenth centuries, the Renaissance was a vast artistic and cultural movement that started in Italy and spread across Europe. French for "rebirth," the Renaissance marks a period of time between the Middle Ages and the modern world in which there was renewed interest in the sciences and art. During this time, a movement called **humanism** began to take shape. In general, humanists relished new ideas and shared a lively interest in the affairs of the world. This was a shift from medieval art that focused on the afterlife and other religious themes.

6 Humanists also emphasized the ability of the individual to think independently, without guidance from higher authorities. Inspired by political, scientific, and philosophical questions, humanists sought to better understand their own world. During this time period, people painted, sculpted, and composed music as never before as they found their own voices and began to express their own ideas. The value that humanism placed on human experience has permanently altered the way people view and judge the world. For instance,

NOTES

humanism's emphasis on intellectual questioning and direct observation is a forerunner to modern scientific methods.

Shakespeare's Humanism

7 Perhaps no Renaissance writer is more well-known than William Shakespeare. More than four hundred years after his death, the poet and playwright is still said to be the world's favorite author. Shakespeare is beloved for both the characters he created and the language he used in his writing. His ability to absorb and transform different kinds of material, ranging from the political issues of his own time to events from Roman and English history, reflects humanist ideals. Shakespeare's tragedies and histories focus on complex individuals who seek to fulfill their full potential while also grappling with painful, difficult dilemmas. At the same time, his comedies are robust with jokes and songs that provide audiences with an escape from their own problems. From Puck to Hamlet and Falstaff to Lady Macbeth, Shakespeare's canon portrays a complete range of human experiences. Young and old, women and men, good and evil, beggars and kings—characters from all walks of life live in Shakespeare's plays.

Ophelia offering fennel and columbines, engraving from *The Illustrated London News*, 1892.

8 Major Concepts

- **Humanism**—To the humanists, human endeavor had dignity and worth in its own right. Influenced by this idea, English writers began to shift their focus from religious concerns and concentrate on secular subjects, such as love, politics, science, and philosophy. Later, in the eighteenth century, a movement called the Enlightenment built on the ideas of individual dignity, rational thought, and secular law.

- **A Bard for the Ages**—William Shakespeare was a singular genius who wrote poems and plays that represent the full flowering of the English

NOTES

Renaissance. His characters, seeking to fulfill their potential, are constantly probing and striving, demonstrating their wit at court, displaying their courage on the battlefield, falling in love and writing poetry, or devising plots to bring about their deepest desires, whether loving or vengeful.

Style and Form

9 **Shakespearean Drama**

- Shakespeare invented little content out of thin air. Instead, he dramatized stories from sources such as Petrarch and Holinshed, often combining elements from multiple accounts of the same story.
- Shakespeare's plays follow a strict format. Each has five acts, and each of those acts contains scenes. Characters express themselves through dialogue as well as soliloquies and monologues. A soliloquy is a speech delivered directly to the audience in which a character reveals his or her innermost thoughts. A monologue is a long speech delivered to another character.
- Subplots, or minor plotlines that support the main plot, are common in Shakespearean drama. Conflicts often arise between characters due to misunderstandings or misinformation that stem from an event that takes place in a subplot.
- Shakespeare's language varies from play to play and sometimes within a play. He is known for writing in iambic pentameter. In this meter, each line has five units, known as feet, and each foot contains an unstressed syllable followed by a stressed syllable. He often uses iambic pentameter to write in blank verse, or writing with a regular meter but without a regular rhyme scheme. He may also include some rhyming couplets for emphasis. However, the language in Shakespeare's plays is not limited to any particular style or meter. He also uses prose, which is ordinary speech without meter or rhyme, when more formal language may seem out of place.
- Sophisticated, intricate language is a trademark of Shakespearean drama. Many plays include elaborate extended metaphors as well as bawdy puns, word play, and double entendres. Humor is always present, even in his tragedies.

10 In addition to featuring characters from all walks of life, Shakespeare's plays drew crowds made up of members from every level of society. Although most of Shakespeare's works were written after Queen Elizabeth I's death, there is proof that she watched several of his plays at court. Elizabeth's successor, James I, even became a patron of Shakespeare's theater company, which was renamed the King's Men. With a focus on individual thought and experiences, it is easy to see why Shakespearean drama and other humanist works were so popular during the Renaissance and continue to be valued. How do the ideas introduced and developed through Renaissance literature continue to inspire audiences today?

Literary Focus: The English Renaissance

Read "Literary Focus: The English Renaissance." After you read, complete the Think Questions below.

THINK QUESTIONS

1. Why was Elizabeth I an important monarch who is still remembered today? Provide two or three reasons, citing evidence from the text to support your response.

2. What were humanists most interested in? Explain, citing evidence from the text to support your response.

3. Based on the information in the reading, explain what a soliloquy is. Why do you think Shakespeare was able to make this form of dramatic speech so popular during the Renaissance specifically? Use text evidence to help support your explanations.

4. Use context clues to determine the meaning of the word ***monarch.*** Write your definition here, along with the specific words or phrases you used to determine the word's meaning. Then check a dictionary to confirm your understanding.

5. What is the meaning of the word ***armada*** as it is used in this text? Write your best definition here, in addition to an explanation of how you arrived at the word's meaning.

Speech to the Troops at Tilbury

ARGUMENTATIVE TEXT
Elizabeth I
1588

Introduction

studysync

In August 1588, King Philip II of Spain sent the huge fleet of warships known as the Spanish Armada to attack and invade England. As ground troops and others assembled at Tilbury, on the bank of the Thames River, in preparation for the expected attack, Elizabeth I (1533–1603), the queen of England, delivered this speech. The Armada was ultimately defeated at sea and never reached England's shores. This text is accompanied by Isaac Oliver's *Rainbow Portrait* of Queen Elizabeth 1, ca. 1600.

". . . We shall shortly have a famous victory over these enemies . . ."

1 My loving people,

2 We have been persuaded by some that are careful of our safety, to take heed how we commit ourselves to armed multitudes, for fear of **treachery;** but I assure you I do not desire to live to distrust my faithful and loving people.

3 Let **tyrants** fear. I have always so behaved myself that, under God, I have placed my chiefest strength and safeguard in the loyal hearts and good-will of my subjects; and therefore I am come amongst you, as you see, at this time, not for my recreation and **disport,** but being resolved, in the midst and heat of the battle, to live and die amongst you all; to lay down for my God, and for my kingdom, and my people, my honour and my blood, even in the dust.

4 I know I have the body of a weak, feeble woman; but I have the heart and stomach of a king, and of a king of England too, and think foul scorn that Parma[1] or Spain, or any prince of Europe, should dare to invade the borders of my realm; to which rather than any dishonour shall grow by me, I myself will take up arms, I myself will be your general, judge, and rewarder of every one of your virtues in the field.

5 I know already, for your forwardness you have deserved rewards and crowns; and We do assure you on a word of a prince, they shall be duly paid. In the mean time, my lieutenant general shall be in my stead, than whom never prince commanded a more noble or worthy subject; not doubting but by your obedience to my general, by your **concord** in the camp, and your **valour** in the field, we shall shortly have a famous victory over these enemies of my God, of my kingdom, and of my people.

NOTES

Skill: Argumentative Text Structure

Elizabeth uses a compare-and-contrast structure to admit her physical weaknesses and display her emotional and intellectual strengths. This structure helps her convince the troops that she is a strong and capable military leader.

1. **Parma** the dukedom of Parma, in northern Italy, an ally of Spain in the effort to invade England

First Read

Read "Speech to the Troops at Tilbury." After you read, complete the Think Questions below.

THINK QUESTIONS

1. Using evidence from the text, infer why the queen is giving this speech instead of a military commander. What character trait does she demonstrate in the speech?

2. What reason would Queen Elizabeth have for saying she does not fear for her safety? Support your response with evidence from the text.

3. What does Queen Elizabeth promise to her audience? What reason would she have for making such a promise? Cite evidence from the text to support your answer.

4. Use context clues to determine the meaning of the word ***disport*** as it is used in "Speech to the Troops at Tilbury." Describe how you determined the meaning. Then look up *disport* in a print or online dictionary to check your inferred definition.

5. Use context clues to determine the meaning of ***tyrants*** as used in "Speech to the Troops at Tilbury." Write your definition of *tyrants* here, and describe how you determined the meaning.

Skill: Argumentative Text Structure

Use the Checklist to analyze Argumentative Text Structure in "Speech to the Troops at Tilbury." Refer to the sample student annotations about Argumentative Text Structure in the text.

••• CHECKLIST FOR ARGUMENTATIVE TEXT STRUCTURE

To critique and evaluate characteristics and structural elements of argumentative texts, note the following:

- ✓ the writer's claim or thesis
- ✓ the evidence the writer uses to support his or her thesis
- ✓ the use of rhetorical appeals
- ✓ counterarguments
- ✓ the conclusion
- ✓ a call to action, or a statement imploring the reader to take action
- ✓ details and signal words that reveal the text's organizing structure

To critique and evaluate characteristics and structural elements of argumentative texts, use the following questions as a guide:

- ✓ Does the author present a clear, arguable thesis? What is that thesis?
- ✓ Are the rhetorical appeals persuasive and appropriate for the intended audience? Why or why not?
- ✓ Does the organizational structure present information in a clear, logical, and persuasive way? Why or why not?
- ✓ How effective is the argument in building to a convincing conclusion, one that leaves the audience with a lasting and memorable impression?
- ✓ How effective is the call to action, and how likely is it to inspire and motivate the intended audience?

Skill: Argumentative Text Structure

Reread paragraph 2 of "Speech to the Troops at Tilbury." Then use the Checklist on the previous page to answer the multiple-choice questions below.

YOUR TURN

1. This question has two parts. First, answer Part A. Then, answer Part B.

Part A: In this excerpt, Queen Elizabeth shows her support for the troops by—

- ○ A. explaining that she does not fear them, even though her advisers think she should.
- ○ B. telling them that she will not indulge in any kind of treachery against them.
- ○ C. assuring them that she will give them plenty of money after they defeat the Spanish enemy.
- ○ D. reminding them that England is in great danger from Spain and may lose its independence.

Part B: Which quote from the excerpt BEST supports the correct response for Part A?

- ○ A. "We have been persuaded by some that are careful for our safety"
- ○ B. "to take heed how we commit ourselves to armed multitudes"
- ○ C. "for fear of treachery"
- ○ D. "I do not desire to live to distrust my faithful and loving people."

Close Read

Reread “Speech to the Troops at Tilbury.” As you reread, complete the Skills Focus questions below. Then use your answers and annotations from the questions to help you complete the Write activity.

SKILLS FOCUS

1. Select a detail in the beginning of the speech that reveals Elizabeth's audience. Explain who her audience is, and describe how she feels about them.
2. Identify a particularly effective structural element in the speech, and explain how Elizabeth's choice to structure her speech this way helps make her argument more convincing.
3. Identify a concession Elizabeth makes, and explain how her inclusion of a counterargument makes the speech more effective.
4. Highlight examples illustrating Elizabeth's humbling herself to the troops. Explain how this approach makes the speech more effective and how this relates to humanism.

WRITE

ARGUMENTATIVE: The great respect and trust Elizabeth has for her troops comes through powerfully when she addresses them at Tilbury. Write an argumentative speech that adapts a similar tone to a subject that you feel strongly about. Express your ideas in strong, clear language to emphasize the importance of your position, and include a call to action.

On Monsieur's Departure

POETRY

Queen Elizabeth I

1582

Introduction

Elizabeth I was the Queen of England from 1558 until her death in 1603. Her reign was known as the Elizabethan era, which is famous for the emergence of the English Renaissance. While serving as queen, the well-educated Elizabeth I wrote numerous poems that seem to be about her life, including "On Monsieur's Departure," in which the speaker expresses the pain of uncertain love.

“I am, and not; I freeze and yet am burned, / Since from myself another self I turned.”

NOTES

I grieve and dare not show my **discontent;**
I love, and yet am forced to seem to hate;
I do, yet dare not say I ever meant;
I seem **stark** mute, but inwardly do prate.[1]
I am, and not; I freeze and yet am burned,
Since from myself another self I turned.

My care is like my shadow in the sun—
Follows me flying, flies when I **pursue** it,
Stands, and lies by me, doth what I have done;
His too familiar care doth make me **rue** it.
No means I find to rid him from my breast,
Till by the end of things it be **suppress**t.

Some gentler passion slide into my mind,
For I am soft, and made of melting snow;
Or be more cruel, Love, and so be kind.
Let me float or sink, be high or low;
Or let me live with some more sweet content,
Or die, and so forget what love e'er meant.

WRITE

LITERARY ANALYSIS: “On Monsieur's Departure” provides a transparent account of the complex emotions accompanying love and loss. What do the emotions of the speaker tell you about the human condition? Consider how figures of speech, such as paradox, contribute to your understanding of the speaker's feelings. Support your writing with evidence from the text.

1. **prate** to talk foolishly or at tedious length about something

Richard III

DRAMA
William Shakespeare
1592

Introduction

studysync

In this famous soliloquy from the opening of Shakespeare's *Richard III,* Richard muses on his circumstances and his plans to seize the throne from his brother through murder, lies, and betrayal.

"Now is the winter of our discontent / Made glorious summer by this son of York."

NOTES

from Act I, Scene i

Characters:
RICHARD, DUKE OF GLOUCESTER: brother to the King Edward IV, afterwards King Richard III

Location: *London. A street.*

Engraving of King Richard III, 1611

1 [*Enter* RICHARD DUKE of GLOUCESTER, *solus*.]

2 GLOUCESTER: Now is the winter of our discontent
3 Made glorious summer by this son of York;[1]
4 And all the clouds that low'r'd upon our house
5 In the deep bosom of the ocean buried.
6 Now are our brows bound with victorious wreaths,
7 Our bruised arms hung up for monuments,
8 Our stern alarums[2] chang'd to merry meetings,

1. **son of York** Richard's brother, King Edward IV, of the York family
2. **stern alarums** alarms, or calls to battle

NOTES

Our dreadful marches to delightful measures.
Grim-visag'd War hath smooth'd his wrinkled front;
And now, in stead of mounting barded steeds
To fright the souls of fearful adversaries,
He capers nimbly in a lady's chamber
To the **lascivious** pleasing of a lute.
But I, that am not shap'd for sportive tricks,
Nor made to court an amorous looking-glass;
I, that am rudely stamp'd, and **want** love's majesty
To strut before a **wanton** ambling nymph;
I, that am curtail'd of this fair proportion,
Cheated of feature by **dissembling** nature,
Deform'd, unfinish'd, sent before my time
Into this breathing world, scarce half made up,
And that so lamely and unfashionable
That dogs bark at me as I halt by them—
Why, I, in this weak piping time of peace,
Have no delight to pass away the time,
Unless to see my shadow in the sun
And **descant** on mine own deformity.
And therefore, since I cannot prove a lover
To entertain these fair well-spoken days,
I am determined to prove a villain
And hate the idle pleasures of these days.
Plots have I laid, inductions dangerous,
By drunken prophecies, libels, and dreams,
To set my brother Clarence and the King
In deadly hate the one against the other;
And if King Edward be as true and just
As I am subtle, false, and treacherous,
This day should Clarence closely be mew'd up
About a prophecy, which says that "G"
Of Edward's heirs the murtherer shall be.
Dive, thoughts, down to my soul, here Clarence comes!

WRITE

CORRESPONDENCE: In the persona of Richard III, write a confessional letter explaining why you choose to be a villain. Use your own words to paraphrase the reasons stated in the soliloquy, but maintain the meaning and logical order of the original text.

Shakespeare:
The World as Stage

ARGUMENTATIVE TEXT
Bill Bryson
2007

Introduction

Known for his distinctly humorous writing style, Bill Bryson (b. 1951) is a highly regarded American author of various nonfiction books on travel, science, language, and other topics. Bryson's biography of William Shakespeare, *Shakespeare: The World as Stage,* focuses on what little is known conclusively about the famous playwright and poet. The excerpt here discusses the Shakespeare authorship debate.

"The presumption is that William Shakespeare of Stratford was, at best, an amiable stooge . . ."

NOTES

Skill: Central or Main Idea

Based on the first sentence, I know that Bryson's main idea will address the Shakespeare debate. Because he is not referring to himself, I can infer that Bryson does not agree that someone other than Shakespeare created these works.

from Chapter 9: Claimants

1 There is an extraordinary—seemingly an **insatiable**—urge on the part of quite a number of people to believe that the plays of William Shakespeare were written by someone other than William Shakespeare. The number of published books suggesting—or more often insisting—as much is estimated now to be well over five thousand.

2 Shakespeare's plays, it is held, so brim with expertise—on law, medicine, statesmanship, court life, military affairs, the bounding main, antiquity, life abroad—that they cannot possibly be the work of a single lightly educated **provincial.** The presumption is that William Shakespeare of Stratford was, at best, an amiable **stooge,** an actor who lent his name as cover for someone of greater talent, someone who could not, for one reason or another, be publicly identified as a playwright.

3 The controversy has been given respectful airing in the highest quarters. PBS, the American television network, in 1996 produced an hour-long documentary **unequivocally** suggesting that Shakespeare probably wasn't Shakespeare. *Harper's Magazine* and the *New York Times* have both devoted generous amounts of space to sympathetically considering the anti-Stratford arguments.[1] The Smithsonian Institution in 2002 held a seminar titled "Who Wrote Shakespeare?" The best-read article in the British magazine *History Today* was one examining the authorship question. Even *Scientific American* entered the fray with an article proposing that the person portrayed in the famous Martin Droeshout engraving[2] might actually be—I weep to say it—Elizabeth I. Perhaps the most extraordinary development of all is that Shakespeare's Globe Theater in London—built as a monument for his plays and with aspirations to be a world-class study center—became, under the

1. **anti-Stratford arguments** the idea that William Shakespeare of Stratford was not the real author of the plays attributed to him
2. **the famous Martin Droeshout engraving** a famous portrait of Shakespeare engraved by Martin Droeshout appearing on the title page of the collection of Shakespeare's plays published in 1623

stewardship of the artistic director Mark Rylance, a kind of clearinghouse for anti-Stratford sentiment.

4 So it needs to be said that nearly all of the anti-Shakespeare sentiment—actually all of it, every bit—involves manipulative scholarship or sweeping misstatements of fact. Shakespeare "never owned a book," a writer for the *New York Times* gravely informed readers in one doubting article in 2002. The statement cannot actually be refuted, for we know nothing about his incidental possessions. But the writer might just as well have suggested that Shakespeare never owned a pair of shoes or pants. For all the evidence tells us, he spent his life unclothed as well as bookless, but it is probable that what is lacking is the evidence, not the apparel or the books.

5 Daniel Wright, a professor at Concordia University in Portland, Oregon, and an active anti-Stratfordian, wrote in *Harper's Magazine* that Shakespeare was "a simple, untutored wool and grain merchant" and "a rather ordinary man who had no connection to the literary world." Such statements can only be characterized as wildly imaginative. Similarly, in the normally **unimpeachable** *History Today*, William D. Rubinstein, a professor at the University of Wales at Aberystwyth, stated in the opening paragraph of his anti-Shakespeare survey: "Of the seventy-five known contemporary documents in which Shakespeare is named, not one concerns his career as an author."

6 That is not even close to being so. In the Master of the Revels' accounts for 1604–1605—that is, the record of plays performed before the king, about as official a record as a record can be—Shakespeare is named seven times as the author of plays performed before James I. He is identified on the title pages as the author of the sonnets and in the dedications of two poems. He is named as author on several quarto[3] editions of his plays, by Francis Meres in *Palladis Tamia*, and by Robert Greene in the *Groat's-Worth of Wit*. John Webster identifies him as one of the great playwrights of the age in his preface to *The White Devil*.

7 The only absence among contemporary records is not of documents connecting Shakespeare to his works but of documents connecting any other human being to them. As the Shakespeare scholar Jonathan Bate has pointed out, virtually no one "in Shakespeare's lifetime or for the first two hundred years after his death expressed the slightest doubt about his authorship."

Excerpted from *Shakespeare: The World as Stage* by Bill Bryson, published by HarperCollins Publishers.

3. **quarto** a book printed on a full sheet that is folded twice to produce four leaves; Shakespeare's works were published in quarto or folio format (a larger, taller book)

NOTES

Skill: Connotation and Denotation

Bryson calls Wright's description of Shakespeare "wildly imaginative." This is an insult because historians write about facts. In fact, *unimpeachable* means "reliable," which tells me Bryson takes issue with Rubinstein's imagination.

Skill: Informational Text Elements

Bryson uses records from that time period as evidence to support his argument. This record lends credibility and refutes assumptions made by the opposition.

First Read

Read *Shakespeare: The World as Stage*. After you read, complete the Think Questions below.

THINK QUESTIONS

1. Why does the author list sources of media coverage of the authorship controversy at the beginning of the selection? Cite evidence from the text to support your answer.

2. What is the author's response to the claim that Shakespeare "never owned a book"? What tone does Bryson use in his response? Support your answer with evidence from the text.

3. How does the author conclude this excerpt? What does that tell you about Bryson's view of the authorship debate? Support your inference with evidence from the text.

4. Use context clues to determine the meaning of the word ***provincial*** as it is used in *Shakespeare: The World as Stage*. Write your definition of *provincial* here, and describe how you determined the meaning.

5. Use your knowledge of word parts and the context clues provided in the text to determine the meaning of ***unimpeachable***. Write your definition of *unimpeachable*, and describe how you determined the meaning.

Skill: Central or Main Idea

Use the Checklist to analyze Central or Main Idea in *Shakespeare: The World as Stage*. Refer to the sample student annotations about Central or Main Idea in the text.

••• CHECKLIST FOR CENTRAL OR MAIN IDEA

To identify two or more central ideas of a text, note the following:

- ✓ key details in each paragraph or section of text, distinguishing what they have in common
- ✓ the main idea in each paragraph or group of paragraphs
- ✓ whether the details contain information that could indicate more than one main idea in a text
    - A science text, for example, may provide information about a specific environment and also a message on ecological awareness.
    - A biography may contain equally important ideas about a person's achievements, influence, and the time period in which the person lives or lived.
- ✓ when each central idea emerges
- ✓ ways the central ideas interact and build on one another

To determine two or more central ideas of a text and analyze their development over the course of the text, including how they interact and build on one another to provide a complex analysis, consider the following questions:

- ✓ What main idea(s) do the details in each paragraph explain or describe?
- ✓ What central or main ideas do all the paragraphs support?
- ✓ How do the central ideas interact and build on one another? How does this affect when they emerge?
- ✓ How might you provide an objective summary of the text? Which details would you include?

Skill:
Central or Main Idea

Reread paragraphs 6 and 7 from *Shakespeare: The World as Stage*. Then use the Checklist on the previous page to answer the multiple-choice questions below.

YOUR TURN

1. Which of the following sentences best summarizes these two paragraphs?

    ○ A. For two hundred years after Shakespeare's death, no one questioned whether he was the original author of his works.

    ○ B. People who choose to question Shakespeare's authorship are free to do so, but they willfully ignore the facts.

    ○ C. Not only is there historical evidence of Shakespeare's authorship, there also is no historical evidence of anyone else having authored these plays.

    ○ D. Scholars continue to question Shakespeare's authorship, based on growing evidence.

2. Which sentence or phrase from the passage does NOT offer clear evidence supporting Bryson's main idea?

    ○ A. "As the Shakespeare scholar Jonathan Bate has pointed out, virtually no one 'in Shakespeare's lifetime or for the first two hundred years after his death expressed the slightest doubt about his authorship.'"

    ○ B. "The only absence among contemporary records is not of documents connecting Shakespeare to his works but of documents connecting any other human being to them."

    ○ C. "In the Master of the Revels' accounts for 1604–1605—that is, the record of plays performed before the king, about as official a record as a record can be—Shakespeare is named seven times as the author of plays performed before James I."

    ○ D. "He is named as author on several quarto editions of his plays, by Francis Meres in *Palladis Tamia*, and by Robert Greene in the *Groat's-Worth of Wit*."

3. In which ways does Bryson mostly develop his main idea?

- ○ A. By providing a study of Shakespeare's works and sharing what he learned with a larger audience
- ○ B. By persuading his audience to become familiar with seventeenth-century literature
- ○ C. By providing evidence of Shakespeare's authorship
- ○ D. By ridiculing those who question Shakespeare's authorship

Skill: Connotation and Denotation

Use the Checklist to analyze Connotation and Denotation in *Shakespeare: The World as Stage*. Refer to the sample student annotations about Connotation and Denotation in the text.

••• CHECKLIST FOR CONNOTATION AND DENOTATION

1. To identify the denotative meanings of words, use the following steps:

    ✓ First, note unfamiliar words and phrases, key words used to describe important individuals, events, and ideas, or words that inspire an emotional reaction.

    ✓ Next, determine and note the denotative meaning of words by consulting a reference material such as a dictionary, glossary, or thesaurus.

    ✓ Finally, analyze nuances in the meaning of words with similar denotations.

2. To better understand the meanings, including connotative meanings, of words and phrases as they are used in a text, use the following questions as a guide:

    ✓ What is the genre or subject of the text? Based on context, what do you think the meaning of the word is intended to be?

    ✓ Is your inference the same or different from the dictionary definition?

    ✓ Does the word create a positive, negative, or neutral emotion?

    ✓ What synonyms or alternative phrasing help you describe the connotative meaning of the word?

3. To determine the meanings, including connotative meanings, of words and phrases as they are used in a text, use the following questions as a guide:

    ✓ What is the denotative meaning of the word? Is that denotative meaning correct in context?

    ✓ What possible positive, neutral, or negative connotations might the word have, depending on context?

    ✓ What textual details signal a particular connotation for the word?

Skill:
Connotation and Denotation

Reread paragraphs 1 and 2 from *Shakespeare: The World as Stage*. Then use the Checklist on the previous page to answer the multiple-choice questions below.

YOUR TURN

1. What is the meaning of *insatiable* as it is used in paragraph 1 of the text?

   - ○ A. limited
   - ○ B. loose
   - ○ C. unexplained
   - ○ D. relentless

2. Read the following dictionary entry:

   insist

   in•sist / in•sist/

   verb

   1. demand something forcefully, not accepting refusal
   2. demand forcefully to have something
   3. persist in doing something even though it is annoying or odd

   Decide which definition and explanation best matches *insist* and its connotations in *Shakespeare: The World as Stage*.

   - ○ A. As used in paragraph 1, *insist* means "to demand something forcefully."
   - ○ B. As used in paragraph 1, *insist* means "to do something even if it is annoying."
   - ○ C. As used in paragraph 1, *insist* means "to not accept a refusal."
   - ○ D. As used in paragraph 1, *insist* means "to do something odd."

3. Which of the following words used in paragraph 2 most denote that the author believes anti-Stratfordians are stubborn with their ideas, despite contrary evidence?

   - ○ A. presumption
   - ○ B. greater talent
   - ○ C. publicly
   - ○ D. insisting

Skill: Informational Text Elements

Use the Checklist to analyze Informational Text Elements in *Shakespeare: The World as Stage*. Refer to the sample student annotations about Informational Text Elements in the text.

••• CHECKLIST FOR INFORMATIONAL TEXT ELEMENTS

To identify a complex set of ideas or sequence of events, note the following:

- ✓ key details in the text that provide information about individuals, events, and ideas
- ✓ interactions between specific individuals, ideas, or events
- ✓ important developments over the course of the text
- ✓ transition words and phrases, such as *because, as a consequence,* or *as a result,* that signal interactions between individuals, events, and ideas.
- ✓ similarities and differences between different types of information in the text by comparing and contrasting facts and opinions

To analyze a complex set of ideas or sequence of events and explain how specific individuals, ideas, or events interact and develop over the course of the text, consider the following questions:

- ✓ How does the order in which ideas or events are presented affect the connections between them?
- ✓ How do specific individuals, ideas, or events interact and develop over the course of the text?
- ✓ What other features, if any, help you analyze the events, ideas, or individuals in the text?

Skill: Informational Text Elements

Reread paragraphs 4 and 5 from *Shakespeare: The World as Stage.* Then use the Checklist on the previous page to answer the multiple-choice questions below.

YOUR TURN

1. When the author states that "The statement cannot actually be refuted," he means—

   - ○ A. to acknowledge the lack of information about Shakespeare.
   - ○ B. there is no evidence, only assumption and opinion to support the notion that Shakespeare never owned a book.
   - ○ C. to persuade the reader to make assumptions about Shakespeare.
   - ○ D. to manipulate scholarly opinion on the subject.

2. What is most likely the reason Bryson provides various examples of anti-Shakespearean sentiment?

   - ○ A. To evoke emotion
   - ○ B. To create confusion among complex ideas
   - ○ C. To educate the reader on the subject matter
   - ○ D. To explain opposing viewpoints and refute claims

3. In paragraph 5, the author tells us that Daniel Wright is a "professor at Concordia University in Portland, Oregon, and an active anti-Stratfordian." What function does this information play within the text?

   - ○ A. To establish Wright as a credible source on Shakespeare
   - ○ B. To include a member of academia in his essay
   - ○ C. To present Wright's professional details in order to later refute his opinion-based claims
   - ○ D. To present a scholarly opinion in support of the author's claim

Close Read

Reread *Shakespeare: The World as Stage*. As you reread, complete the Skills Focus questions below. Then use your answers and annotations from the questions to help you complete the Write activity.

SKILLS FOCUS

1. What is Bryson's central idea in paragraph 4? How does Bryson's tone in the paragraph help develop the central idea? Highlight evidence to support your ideas and make annotations to write your response.

2. In the second paragraph, what does Bryson mean when he refers to Shakespeare as a "lightly educated provincial"? What connotation does that phrase have, and what does it tell you about Bryson's viewpoint? Highlight evidence in the text and make annotations to explain the phrase.

3. Why does Bryson list the professions of Daniel Wright and William D. Rubinstein in paragraph 5? What is his purpose for including the long list of media outlets in paragraph 3? How do these details support his central idea? Highlight evidence from the text, and make annotations to support your ideas.

4. Identify an opposing opinion Bryson considers and the argument he forges in response. Explain how his rebuttal contributes to the effectiveness of the text. How does it support his main idea? Cite evidence from the text to support your answer.

5. What are the truths about Shakespeare and the scholarship surrounding Shakespeare that the author is defending in this excerpt? Why does this truth matter?

WRITE

RHETORICAL ANALYSIS: Bryson takes a strong, transparent view on the subject of Shakespearean authorship from the beginning of the excerpt and maintains it throughout. What is Bryson's main idea regarding the authorship debate? What are the key pieces of evidence and informational text elements he uses to make his point? Cite specific evidence from the text to support your claim.

Hamlet and His Problems

ARGUMENTATIVE TEXT
T. S. Eliot
1919

Introduction

Written in 1919, this essay by writer T. S. Eliot (1888–1965) urges critics to analyze *Hamlet* through the lens of New Criticism, which views a text outside its history or performance. Eliot's essay addresses the concept of finding the "objective correlative," a technique used to evoke emotion in an audience.

"The grounds of *Hamlet's* failure are not immediately obvious."

NOTES

1 Few critics have even admitted that *Hamlet* the play is the primary problem, and Hamlet the character only secondary. And Hamlet the character has had an especial temptation for that most dangerous type of critic: the critic with a mind which is naturally of the creative order, but which through some

T. S. Eliot, 1951

weakness in creative power exercises itself in criticism instead. These minds often find in Hamlet a **vicarious** existence for their own artistic realization. Such a mind had Goethe, who made of Hamlet a Werther; and such had Coleridge, who made of Hamlet a Coleridge; and probably neither of these men in writing about Hamlet remembered that his first business was to study a work of art. The kind of criticism that Goethe and Coleridge produced, in writing of Hamlet, is the most misleading kind possible. For they both possessed unquestionable critical insight, and both make their critical aberrations the more plausible by the substitution—of their own Hamlet for Shakespeare's—which their creative gift effects. We should be thankful that Walter Pater did not fix his attention on this play.

2 Two recent writers, Mr. J. M. Robertson and Professor Stoll of the University of Minnesota, have issued small books which can be praised for moving in the other direction. Mr. Stoll performs a service in recalling to our attention the

NOTES

labours of the critics of the seventeenth and eighteenth centuries, observing that they knew less about psychology than more recent Hamlet critics, but they were nearer in spirit to Shakespeare's art; and as they insisted on the importance of the effect of the whole rather than on the importance of the leading character, they were nearer, in their old-fashioned way, to the secret of dramatic art in general.

3 *Qua*[1] work of art, the work of art cannot be interpreted; there is nothing to interpret; we can only criticize it according to standards, in comparison to other works of art; and for "interpretation" the chief task is the presentation of relevant historical facts which the reader is not assumed to know. Mr. Robertson points out, very pertinently, how critics have failed in their "interpretation" of *Hamlet* by ignoring what ought to be very obvious: that *Hamlet* is a **stratification,** that it represents the efforts of a series of men, each making what he could out of the work of his predecessors. The *Hamlet* of Shakespeare will appear to us very differently if, instead of treating the whole action of the play as due to Shakespeare's design, we perceive his *Hamlet* to be superposed upon much cruder material which persists even in the final form.

4 We know that there was an older play by Thomas Kyd, that extraordinary dramatic (if not poetic) genius who was in all probability the author of two plays so dissimilar as the *Spanish Tragedy* and *Arden of Feversham;* and what this play was like we can guess from three clues: from the *Spanish Tragedy* itself, from the tale of Belleforest upon which Kyd's *Hamlet* must have been based, and from a version acted in Germany in Shakespeare's lifetime which bears strong evidence of having been adapted from the earlier, not from the later, play. From these three sources it is clear that in the earlier play the motive was a revenge-motive simply; that the action or delay is caused, as in the *Spanish Tragedy*, solely by the difficulty of assassinating a monarch surrounded by guards; and that the "madness" of Hamlet was feigned in order to escape suspicion, and successfully. In the final play of Shakespeare, on the other hand, there is a motive which is more important than that of revenge, and which explicitly "blunts" the latter; the delay in revenge is unexplained on grounds of necessity or expediency; and the effect of the "madness" is not to lull but to arouse the king's suspicion. The alteration is not complete enough, however, to be convincing. Furthermore, there are verbal parallels so close to the *Spanish Tragedy* as to leave no doubt that in places Shakespeare was merely *revising* the text of Kyd. And finally there are unexplained scenes—the Polonius-Laertes and the Polonius-Reynaldo scenes—for which there is little excuse; these scenes are not in the verse style of Kyd, and not beyond doubt in the style of Shakespeare. These Mr. Robertson believes to be scenes in the original play of Kyd reworked by a

1. ***qua*** (Latin) as being

NOTES

third hand, perhaps Chapman, before Shakespeare touched the play. And he concludes, with very strong show of reason, that the original play of Kyd was, like certain other revenge plays, in two parts of five acts each. The upshot of Mr. Robertson's examination is, we believe, irrefragable: that Shakespeare's *Hamlet,* so far as it is Shakespeare's, is a play dealing with the effect of a mother's guilt upon her son, and that Shakespeare was unable to impose this motive successfully upon the **"intractable"** material of the old play.

5 Of the intractability there can be no doubt. So far from being Shakespeare's masterpiece, the play is most certainly an artistic failure. In several ways the play is puzzling, and disquieting as is none of the others. Of all the plays it is the longest and is possibly the one on which Shakespeare spent most pains; and yet he has left in it **superfluous** and inconsistent scenes which even hasty revision should have noticed. The versification is variable. Lines like:

6 Look, the morn, in russet mantle clad,
Walks o'er the dew of yon high eastern hill,

7 are of the Shakespeare of *Romeo and Juliet.* The lines in Act v. sc. ii.,

8 Sir, in my heart there was a kind of fighting
That would not let me sleep. . .
Up from my cabin,
My sea-gown scarf'd about me, in the dark
Grop'd I to find out them: had my desire;
Finger'd their packet;

9 are of his quite mature. Both workmanship and thought are in an unstable condition. We are surely justified in attributing the play, with that other profoundly interesting play of "intractable" material and astonishing versification, *Measure for Measure,* to a period of crisis, after which follow the tragic successes which culminate in *Coriolanus. Coriolanus* may be not as "interesting" as *Hamlet,* but it is, with *Antony and Cleopatra,* Shakespeare's most assured artistic success. And probably more people have thought *Hamlet* a work of art because they found it interesting, than have found it interesting because it is a work of art. It is the "Mona Lisa" of literature.

10 The grounds of *Hamlet's* failure are not immediately obvious. Mr. Robertson is undoubtedly correct in concluding that the essential emotion of the play is the feeling of a son towards a guilty mother:

11 "[Hamlet's] tone is that of one who has suffered tortures on the score of his mother's degradation. . . . The guilt of a mother is an almost intolerable motive for drama, but it had to be maintained and emphasized to supply a psychological solution, or rather a hint of one."

NOTES

12 This, however, is by no means the whole story. It is not merely the "guilt of a mother" that cannot be handled as Shakespeare handled the suspicion of Othello, the infatuation of Antony, or the pride of Coriolanus. The subject might conceivably have expanded into a tragedy like these, intelligible, self-complete, in the sunlight. *Hamlet*, like the sonnets, is full of some stuff that the writer could not drag to light, contemplate, or manipulate into art. And when we search for this feeling, we find it, as in the sonnets, very difficult to localize. You cannot point to it in the speeches; indeed, if you examine the two famous soliloquies you see the versification of Shakespeare, but a content which might be claimed by another, perhaps by the author of the *Revenge of Bussy d'Ambois,* Act v. sc. i. We find Shakespeare's *Hamlet* not in the action, not in any quotations that we might select, so much as in an unmistakable tone which is unmistakably not in the earlier play.

13 The only way of expressing emotion in the form of art is by finding an "objective correlative"; in other words, a set of objects, a situation, a chain of events which shall be the formula of that *particular* emotion; such that when the external facts, which must terminate in sensory experience, are given, the emotion is immediately evoked. If you examine any of Shakespeare's more successful tragedies, you will find this exact equivalence; you will find that the state of mind of Lady Macbeth walking in her sleep has been communicated to you by a skilful accumulation of imagined sensory impressions; the words of Macbeth on hearing of his wife's death strike us as if, given the sequence of events, these words were automatically released by the last event in the series. The artistic "inevitability" lies in this complete adequacy of the external to the emotion; and this is precisely what is deficient in *Hamlet*. Hamlet (the man) is dominated by an emotion which is inexpressible, because it is in excess of the facts as they appear. And the supposed identity of Hamlet with his author is genuine to this point: that Hamlet's bafflement at the absence of objective equivalent to his feelings is a prolongation of the bafflement of his creator in the face of his artistic problem. Hamlet is up against the difficulty that his disgust is occasioned by his mother, but that his mother is not an adequate equivalent for it; his disgust envelops and exceeds her. It is thus a feeling which he cannot understand; he cannot objectify it, and it therefore remains to poison life and obstruct action. None of the possible actions can satisfy it; and nothing that Shakespeare can do with the plot can express Hamlet for him. And it must be noticed that the very nature of the *données*[2] of the problem precludes objective equivalence. To have heightened the criminality of Gertrude would have been to provide the formula for a totally different emotion in Hamlet; it is just *because* her character is so negative and insignificant that she arouses in Hamlet the feeling which she is incapable of representing.

2. ***données*** (French) basic facts

NOTES

14 The "madness" of Hamlet lay to Shakespeare's hand; in the earlier play a simple **ruse,** and to the end, we may presume, understood as a ruse by the audience. For Shakespeare it is less than madness and more than feigned. The levity of Hamlet, his repetition of phrase, his puns, are not part of a deliberate plan of dissimulation, but a form of emotional relief. In the character Hamlet it is the buffoonery of an emotion which can find no outlet in action; in the dramatist it is the buffoonery of an emotion which he cannot express in art. The intense feeling, ecstatic or terrible, without an object or exceeding its object, is something which every person of sensibility has known; it is doubtless a study to pathologists. It often occurs in adolescence: the ordinary person puts these feelings to sleep, or trims down his feeling to fit the business world; the artist keeps it alive by his ability to intensify the world to his emotions. The Hamlet of Laforgue is an adolescent; the Hamlet of Shakespeare is not, he has not that explanation and excuse. We must simply admit that here Shakespeare tackled a problem which proved too much for him. Why he attempted it at all is an insoluble puzzle; under compulsion of what experience he attempted to express the inexpressibly horrible, we cannot ever know. We need a great many facts in his biography; and we should like to know whether, and when, and after or at the same time as what personal experience, he read Montaigne, II. xii., *Apologie de Raimond Sebond*. We should have, finally, to know something which is by hypothesis unknowable, for we assume it to be an experience which, in the manner indicated, exceeded the facts. We should have to understand things which Shakespeare did not understand himself.

WRITE

EXPLANATORY: In the essay "Hamlet and His Problems," T. S. Eliot makes the claim that Shakespeare's play *Hamlet* is "an artistic failure." Why does he make this claim? What ideas and examples does he use to support this claim? Write a response in which you answer these questions. Remember to use evidence from the text to support your response.

Hamlet

(Scenes from Acts I, II, and III)

DRAMA
William Shakespeare
1601

Introduction

The Tragedy of Hamlet, Prince of Denmark by William Shakespeare (ca. 1564–1616) is a vivid portrayal of madness, rich with themes of treachery and revenge. His father, the king's, death and his mother's immediate remarriage to his uncle throws Hamlet into existential turmoil—a struggle for personal meaning and grueling internal strife that threatens to consume him. A ghost, once played by Shakespeare himself around 1602, visits the prince. Hamlet's soliloquies, exemplifying the best of Shakespeare's eloquent and clever language, raise unanswerable questions and explore the reality of being human in one of the greatest plays ever written.

"To be, or not to be, that is the question . . ."

1 *Hamlet has returned home from studying in Wittenberg to attend his father's funeral. Still in deep mourning, Hamlet is appalled by his mother's hasty remarriage to the dead king's brother, who has assumed the throne and persists in calling him "son." The circumstances drive Hamlet to voice his first passionate soliloquy.*

from Act I, scene ii

Hamlet: son to the late King Hamlet, and nephew to the present king
Claudius: King of Denmark
Gertrude: Queen of Denmark, and mother to Hamlet
Polonius: Lord Chamberlain
Laertes: son to Polonius

Location: Elsinore, the castle

2 KING: Take thy fair hour, Laertes, time be thine,
3 And thy best graces spend it at thy will!
4 But now, my cousin Hamlet, and my son—

5 HAMLET: *[Aside]* A little more than kin, and less than kind.

6 KING: How is it that the clouds still hang on you?

7 HAMLET: Not so, my lord, I am too much in the sun.

8 QUEEN: Good Hamlet, cast thy nighted color off,
9 And let thine eye look like a friend on Denmark.
10 Do not for ever with thy vailed lids
11 Seek for thy noble father in the dust.
12 Thou know'st 'tis common, all that lives must die,
13 Passing through nature to eternity.

14 HAMLET: Ay, madam, it is common.

NOTES

Skill:
Dramatic Elements and Structure

The aside reveals Hamlet's negative feelings toward his uncle that motivate him to want to avenge his father's death later in the play.

Also, the author's use of an aside creates a relationship between the audience and Hamlet.

NOTES

QUEEN: If it be,
Why seems it so particular with thee?

HAMLET: Seems, madam? Nay, it is, I know not "seems."
'Tis not alone my inky cloak, good mother,
Nor customary suits of solemn black,
Nor windy suspiration of forc'd breath,
No, nor the fruitful river in the eye,
Nor the dejected havior of the visage,
Together with all forms, moods, shapes of grief,
That can denote me truly. These indeed seem,
For they are actions that a man might play,
But I have that within which passes show,
These but the **trappings** and the suits of woe.

KING: 'Tis sweet and commendable in your nature, Hamlet,
To give these mourning duties to your father.
But you must know your father lost a father,
That father lost, lost his, and the survivor bound
In **filial** obligation for some term
To do obsequious sorrow. But to persever
In obstinate condolement is a course
Of impious stubbornness, 'tis unmanly grief,
It shows a will most incorrect to heaven,
A heart unfortified, or mind impatient,
An understanding simple and unschool'd:
For what we know must be, and is as common
As any the most vulgar thing to sense,
Why should we in our peevish opposition
Take it to heart? Fie, 'tis a fault to heaven,
A fault against the dead, a fault to nature,
To reason most absurd, whose common theme
Is death of fathers, and who still hath cried,
From the first corse till he that died to-day,
"This must be so." We pray you, throw to earth
This unprevailing woe, and think of us
As of a father, for let the world take note
You are the most immediate to our throne,
And with no less nobility of love
Than that which dearest father bears his son
Do I impart toward you. For your intent
In going back to school in Wittenberg,
It is most **retrograde** to our desire,
And we beseech you, bend you to remain

Here in the cheer and comfort of our eye,
Our chiefest courtier, cousin, and our son.

QUEEN: Let not thy mother lose her prayers, Hamlet,
I pray thee stay with us, go not to Wittenberg.

HAMLET: I shall in all my best obey you, madam.

KING: Why, 'tis a loving and a fair reply.
Be as ourself in Denmark. Madam, come.
This gentle and unforc'd accord of Hamlet
Sits smiling to my heart, in grace whereof,
No jocund health that Denmark drinks to-day,
But the great cannon to the clouds shall tell,
And the King's rouse the heaven shall bruit again,
Respeaking earthly thunder. Come away.

[Flourish. Exeunt all but HAMLET.]

HAMLET: O that this too too solid flesh would melt,
Thaw and resolve itself into a dew!
Or that the Everlasting had not fix'd
His canon 'gainst self-slaughter! O God, God,
How weary, stale, flat and unprofitable
Seem to me all the uses of this world!
Fie on't, ah fie! 'tis an unweeded garden
That grows to seed, things rank and gross in nature
Possess it merely. That it should come to this!
But two months dead, nay, not so much, not two.
So excellent a king, that was to this
Hyperion[1]—to a satyr,[2] so loving to my mother
That he might not beteem the winds of heaven
Visit her face too roughly. Heaven and earth,
Must I remember? Why, she would hang on him
As if increase of appetite had grown
By what it fed on, and yet, within a month—
Let me not think on't! Frailty, thy name is woman!—
A little month, or ere those shoes were old
With which she followed my poor father's body,
Like Niobe, all tears—why, she, even she—
O, God, a beast that wants discourse of reason

NOTES

Skill: Dramatic Elements and Structure

Alone on stage, Hamlet wishes he were dead because he thinks his life has lost all meaning. His soliloquy and the stage direction work together to reveal how disgusted he is with his mother's marriage to his uncle.

1. **Hyperion** the sun god
2. **satyr** in Greek mythology, a lustful, drunken god of the woods, represented as a half man-half horse or goat

NOTES

93 Would have mourn'd longer—married with my uncle,
94 My father's brother, but no more like my father
95 Than I to Hercules. Within a month,
96 Ere yet the salt of most unrighteous tears
97 Had left the flushing in her galled eyes,
98 She married—O most wicked speed: to post
99 With such dexterity to incestuous sheets,
100 It is not, nor it cannot come to good,
101 But break my heart, for I must hold my tongue.

from Act II, scene ii

102 *Hamlet has been visited by an apparition claiming to be the ghost of his father, who urges Hamlet to avenge his father's murder. Hamlet swears he will obey but hesitates. Watching a group of traveling players perform the murder of Priam, king of Troy, Hamlet compares one actor's passionate portrayal of Hecuba, Priam's grieving widow, to his own inaction.*

Hamlet and His Father's Ghost

103 HAMLET: O, what a rogue and peasant slave am I!
104 Is it not monstrous that this player here,
105 But in a fiction, in a dream of passion,
106 Could force his soul so to his own conceit
107 That from her working all his visage wann'd,
108 Tears in his eyes, distraction in his aspect,
109 A broken voice, an' his whole function suiting
110 With forms to his conceit? And all for nothing,
111 For Hecuba!
112 What's Hecuba to him, or he to Hecuba,
113 That he should weep for her? What would he do
114 Had he the motive and the cue for passion
115 That I have? He would drown the stage with tears,
116 And cleave the general ear with horrid speech,

NOTES

Make mad the guilty, and appall the free,
Confound the ignorant, and amaze indeed
The very faculties of eyes and ears. Yet I,
A dull and muddy-mettled rascal, peak[3]
Like John-a-dreams,[4] unpregnant of[5] my cause,
And can say nothing; no, not for a king,
Upon whose property and most dear life
A damn'd defeat was made. Am I a coward?
Who calls me villain, breaks my pate across,
Plucks off my beard, and blows it in my face,
Tweaks me by the nose, gives me the lie i' the throat
As deep as to the lungs? Who does me this?
Hah, 'swounds, I should take it; for it cannot be
But I am pigeon-liver'd, and lack gall
To make oppression bitter, or ere this
I should 'a' fatted all the region kites
With this slave's offal. Bloody, bawdy villain!
Remorseless, treacherous, lecherous, kindless villain!
Why, what an ass am I! This is most brave,
That I, the son of a dear father murthered,
Prompted to my revenge by heaven and hell,
Must, like a whore unpack my heart with words,
And fall a-cursing like a very drab,
A stallion. Fie upon't, foh!
About, my brains! Hum—I have heard
That guilty creatures sitting at a play
Have by the very cunning of the scene
Been struck so to the soul, that presently
They have proclaim'd their malefactions:
For murther, though it have no tongue, will speak
With most miraculous organ. I'll have these players
Play something like the murther of my father
Before mine uncle. I'll observe his looks,
I'll tent[6] him to the quick. If 'a do blench,[7]
I know my course. The spirit that I have seen
May be the dev'l, and the dev'l hath power
T' assume a pleasing shape, yea, and perhaps,
Out of my weakness and my melancholy,
As he is very potent with such spirits,
Abuses me to damn me. I'll have grounds

3. **peak** to mope
4. **John-a-dreams** a nickname for a daydreamer
5. **unpregnant of** unquickened, or unmoved, by
6. **tent** probe
7. **blench** flinch

NOTES

157 More relative than this—the play's the thing
158 Wherein I'll catch the conscience of the King.

from Act III, scene i

159 *Hamlet has been acting mad in front of his family and the court. The King and Polonius hope that Hamlet's strange behavior stems from his love for Polonius's daughter, Ophelia, and they spy on the young couple in order to confirm their suspicions. While hidden, they catch Hamlet in a private moment of anguished contemplation.*

160 HAMLET: To be, or not to be, that is the question:
161 Whether 'tis nobler in the mind to suffer
162 The slings and arrows of outrageous fortune,
163 Or to take arms against a sea of troubles,
164 And by opposing, end them. To die, to sleep—
165 No more, and by a sleep to say we end
166 The heart-ache and the thousand natural shocks
167 That flesh is heir to; 'tis a consummation
168 Devoutly to be wish'd. To die, to sleep—
169 To sleep, perchance to dream—ay, there's the rub,
170 For in that sleep of death what dreams may come,
171 When we have shuffled off this mortal coil,
172 Must give us pause; there's the respect
173 That makes calamity of so long life:
174 For who would bear the whips and scorns of time,
175 Th' oppressor's wrong, the proud man's contumely,
176 The pangs of despis'd love, the law's delay,
177 The **insolence** of office, and the spurns
178 That patient merit of th' unworthy takes,
179 When he himself might his quietus make
180 With a bare bodkin;[8] who would fardels[9] bear,
181 To grunt and sweat under a weary life,
182 But that the dread of something after death,
183 The undiscover'd country, from whose bourn
184 No traveller returns, puzzles the will,
185 And makes us rather bear those ills we have,
186 Than fly to others that we know not of?
187 Thus conscience does make cowards of us all,
188 And thus the native hue of resolution
189 Is sicklied o'er with the pale cast of thought,
190 And enterprises of great pith and moment

Skill: Media

The film shows Hamlet looking at the ocean. His words are heard before he is on screen. He holds a dagger when he says "end them." The film makes Hamlet's suicidal thoughts clearer than I originally read in Shakespeare's words.

8. **bare bodkin** a mere dagger
9. **fardel** a burden in the form of a bundle

NOTES

191 With this regard their currents turn awry,
192 And lose the name of action.—Soft you now,
193 The fair Ophelia!—Nymph, in thy orisons[10]
194 Be all my sins remembered.

195 OPHELIA: Good my lord,
196 How does your honor for this many a day?

197 HAMLET: I humbly thank you. Well, well, well.

198 OPHELIA: My lord, I have remembrances of yours
199 That I have longèd long to redeliver.
200 I pray you now receive them.

201 HAMLET: No, not I. I never gave you aught.

202 OPHELIA: My honored lord, you know right well you did,
203 And with them, words of so sweet breath composed
204 As made the things more rich. Their perfume lost,
205 Take these again, for to the noble mind
206 Rich gifts wax poor when givers prove unkind.
207 There, my lord.

208 HAMLET: Ha, ha, are you honest?

209 OPHELIA: My lord?

210 HAMLET: Are you fair?

211 OPHELIA: What means your lordship?

212 HAMLET: That if you be honest and fair, your honesty should admit no discourse to your beauty.

213 OPHELIA: Could beauty, my lord, have better commerce than with honesty?

214 HAMLET: Ay, truly, for the power of beauty will sooner transform honesty from what it is to a bawd than the force of honesty can translate beauty into his likeness. This was sometime a paradox, but now the time gives it proof. I did love you once.

215 OPHELIA: Indeed, my lord, you made me believe so.

10. **orison** a prayer

NOTES

216 HAMLET: You should not have believed me, for virtue cannot so inoculate our old stock but we shall relish of it. I loved you not.

217 OPHELIA: I was the more deceived.

218 HAMLET: Get thee to a nunnery. Why wouldst thou be a breeder of sinners? I am myself indifferent honest, but yet I could accuse me of such things that it were better my mother had not borne me.

219 I am very proud, revengeful, ambitious, with more offences at my beck than I have thoughts to put them in, imagination to give them shape, or time to act them in. What should such fellows as I do crawling between earth and heaven? We are arrant knaves, all. Believe none of us. Go thy ways to a nunnery. Where's your father?

220 OPHELIA: At home, my lord.

221 HAMLET: Let the doors be shut upon him, that he may play the fool no where but in 's own house. Farewell.

222 OPHELIA: O, help him, you sweet heavens!

223 HAMLET: If thou dost marry, I'll give thee this plague for thy dowry. Be thou as chaste as ice, as pure as snow, thou shalt not escape calumny. Get thee to a nunnery, go. Farewell. Or, if thou wilt needs marry, marry a fool, for wise men know well enough what monsters you make of them. To a nunnery, go, and quickly too. Farewell.

224 OPHELIA: Heavenly powers, restore him!

225 HAMLET: I have heard of your paintings too, well enough. God has given you one face and you make yourselves another. You jig and amble, and you lisp, you nickname God's creatures and make your wantonness your ignorance. Go to, I'll no more on 't. It hath made me mad. I say, we will have no more marriages. Those that are married already, all but one, shall live. The rest shall keep as they are. To a nunnery, go.

226 [*Exit HAMLET*.]

227 OPHELIA: Oh, what a noble mind is here o'erthrown!—
228 The courtier's, soldier's, scholar's, eye, tongue, sword,
229 Th' expectancy and rose of the fair state,
230 The glass of fashion and the mould of form,
231 Th' observed of all observers, quite, quite down!
232 And I, of ladies most deject and wretched,
233 That sucked the honey of his music vows,

NOTES

Now see that noble and most sovereign reason
Like sweet bells jangled, out of tune and harsh;
That unmatched form and feature of blown youth
Blasted with ecstasy. Oh, woe is me,
T' have seen what I have seen, see what I see!

from Act III, scene iii

A room in the castle.

[Enter KING, ROSENCRANTZ, and GUILDENSTERN.]

KING: I like him not; nor stands it safe with us
To let his madness range. Therefore prepare you;
I your commission will forthwith dispatch,
And he to England shall along with you:
The terms of our estate may not endure
Hazard so near us as doth hourly grow
Out of his lunacies.

GUILDENSTERN: We will ourselves provide:
Most holy and religious fear it is
To keep those many many bodies safe
That live and feed upon your majesty.

ROSENCRANTZ: The single and peculiar life is bound,
With all the strength and armour of the mind,
To keep itself from 'noyance; but much more
That spirit upon whose weal depend and rest
The lives of many. The cease of majesty
Dies not alone; but like a gulf doth draw
What's near it with it: it is a massy wheel,
Fix'd on the summit of the highest mount,
To whose huge spokes ten thousand lesser things
Are mortis'd and adjoin'd; which, when it falls,
Each small annexment, petty consequence,
Attends the **boisterous** ruin. Never alone
Did the king sigh, but with a general groan.

KING: Arm you, I pray you, to this speedy voyage;
For we will fetters put upon this fear,
Which now goes too free-footed.

ROSENCRANTZ and GUILDENSTERN: We will haste us.

[Exeunt ROSENCRANTZ and GUILDENSTERN.]

NOTES

[Enter POLONIUS.]

POLONIUS: My lord, he's going to his mother's closet:
Behind the arras I'll convey myself
To hear the process; I'll warrant she'll tax him home:
And, as you said, and wisely was it said,
'Tis meet that some more audience than a mother,
Since nature makes them partial, should o'erhear
The speech, of vantage. Fare you well, my liege:
I'll call upon you ere you go to bed,
And tell you what I know.

KING: Thanks, dear my lord.

[Exit POLONIUS.]

Skill: Language, Style, and Audience

The king describes the murder of his brother as so "rank" that the smell rises to heaven. But "my offence is rank" can also mean that the king's "offence," or crime, is to achieve rank.

O, my offence is rank, it smells to heaven;
It hath the primal eldest curse upon't,—
A brother's murder!—Pray can I not,
Though inclination be as sharp as will:
My stronger guilt defeats my strong intent;
And, like a man to double business bound,
I stand in pause where I shall first begin,
And both neglect. What if this cursed hand
Were thicker than itself with brother's blood,—
Is there not rain enough in the sweet heavens
To wash it white as snow? Whereto serves mercy
But to confront the visage of offence?
And what's in prayer but this twofold force,—
To be forestalled ere we come to fall,
Or pardon'd being down? Then I'll look up;
My fault is past. But, O, what form of prayer
Can serve my turn? Forgive me my foul murder!—
That cannot be; since I am still possess'd
Of those effects for which I did the murder,—
My crown, mine own ambition, and my queen.
May one be pardon'd and retain the offence?
In the corrupted currents of this world
Offence's gilded hand may shove by justice;
And oft 'tis seen the wicked prize itself
Buys out the law; but 'tis not so above;
There is no shuffling;—there the action lies
In his true nature; and we ourselves compell'd,
Even to the teeth and forehead of our faults,
To give in evidence. What then? what rests?

NOTES

Try what repentance can: what can it not?
Yet what can it when one cannot repent?
O wretched state! O bosom black as death!
O limed soul, that, struggling to be free,
Art more engag'd! Help, angels! Make assay:
Bow, stubborn knees; and, heart, with strings of steel,
Be soft as sinews of the new-born babe!
All may be well.

[Retires and kneels.]

[Enter Hamlet.]

HAMLET: Now might I do it pat, now he is praying;
And now I'll do't;—and so he goes to heaven;
And so am I reveng'd.—that would be scann'd:
A villain kills my father; and for that,
I, his sole son, do this same villain send
To heaven.
O, this is hire and salary, not revenge.
He took my father grossly, full of bread;
With all his crimes broad blown, as flush as May;
And how his audit stands, who knows save heaven?
But in our circumstance and course of thought,
'Tis heavy with him: and am I, then, reveng'd,
To take him in the purging of his soul,
When he is fit and season'd for his passage?
No.
Up, sword, and know thou a more horrid hent:
When he is drunk asleep; or in his rage;
Or in the incestuous pleasure of his bed;
At gaming, swearing; or about some act
That has no relish of salvation in't;—
Then trip him, that his heels may kick at heaven;
And that his soul may be as damn'd and black
As hell, whereto it goes. My mother stays:
This physic but prolongs thy sickly days.

[Exit.]

[The king rises and advances.]

KING: My words fly up, my thoughts remain below:
Words without thoughts never to heaven go.

[Exit.]

First Read

Read *Hamlet* (Scenes from Acts I, II, and III). After you read, complete the Think Questions below.

THINK QUESTIONS

1. In Act I, how do King Claudius and Queen Gertrude try to reason with Hamlet? What does Hamlet's soliloquy suggest about his response to their reasoning? Cite evidence from the text to support your response.

2. In Act II, what key comparison does Hamlet draw between himself and the players, confirming that he is a coward? Cite evidence from the text to support your answer.

3. In Act III, scene i, what does Hamlet mean when he says, "To be, or not to be, that is the question"? Cite evidence from the text to support your answer.

4. Review the king's lines in Act I, scene ii, that begin, "'Tis sweet and commendable . . ." Use context to determine the meaning of the word ***filial*** as it is used in the fifth line. Explain how context helped you determine the meaning of the word.

5. Use context clues to determine a preliminary definition of ***retrograde.*** Write your definition here, and then verify your preliminary definition by checking a dictionary.

Skill: Dramatic Elements and Structure

Use the Checklist to analyze Dramatic Elements and Structure in *Hamlet* (Scenes from Acts I, II, and III). Refer to the sample student annotations about Dramatic Elements and Structure in the text.

••• CHECKLIST FOR DRAMATIC ELEMENTS AND STRUCTURE

To determine the author's choices regarding the development of a drama, note the following:

- ✓ the names of all the characters, how they are introduced, and their relationships with one another
- ✓ character development, including personality traits, motivations, decisions each character makes, and the actions they take
- ✓ the setting(s) of the story and how it influences the characters and the events of the plot
- ✓ how character choices and dialogue affect the plot
- ✓ the stage directions and how they are used to reveal character and plot development

To analyze the impact of the author's choices regarding how to develop and relate elements of a story or drama, consider the following questions:

- ✓ How does the order of events in the play affect the development of the drama?
- ✓ How are characters introduced, and what does it reveal about them?
- ✓ In what ways do the characters change over the course of the drama?
- ✓ How do the choices the characters make help advance the plot?
- ✓ How does the setting affect the characters and plot?
- ✓ How do the characters' actions help develop the theme or message of the play?

Skill: Dramatic Elements and Structure

Reread lines 102–126 from *Hamlet* (Scenes from Acts I, II, and III). Then use the Checklist on the previous page to answer the multiple-choice questions below.

YOUR TURN

1. This scene is from the second act of Hamlet. The author's choice to use a soliloquy at this point in the play helps advance the plot by—

    ○ A. making the audience approve of Hamlet's plan to get revenge on his family later in the play.
    ○ B. allowing Hamlet's family to find out what he is plotting, which enables them to foil his plan.
    ○ C. creating a mood of forgiveness that will affect Hamlet's actions toward his uncle and mother.
    ○ D. creating tension in the rising action of the play as the audience learns of Hamlet's plan for revenge.

2. The author's choice to use a soliloquy in this part of the play is effective because it—

    ○ A. leaves no question in the audience's mind that Hamlet, alone on stage, is revealing his inner thoughts and feelings.
    ○ B. allows Hamlet to be alone on stage so he can tell the audience directly that he enjoys putting on plays.
    ○ C. gives Hamlet a chance to get the audience to react to the claim that he is a rogue and a villain.
    ○ D. gives other actors a chance to be offstage so they can prepare for future scenes.

Skill: Language, Style, and Audience

Use the Checklist to analyze Language, Style, and Audience in *Hamlet* (Scenes from Acts I, II, and III). Refer to the sample student annotations about Language, Style, and Audience in the text.

••• CHECKLIST FOR LANGUAGE, STYLE, AND AUDIENCE

To determine an author's style and possible intended audience, do the following:

- ✓ Identify and define any unfamiliar words or phrases that have multiple meanings.
- ✓ Identify language that is particularly fresh, engaging, or beautiful.
- ✓ Analyze the surrounding words and phrases as well as the context in which the specific words are being used.
- ✓ Note the audience—both intended and unintended—and possible reactions to the author's word choice and style.
- ✓ Examine your reaction to the author's word choice and how the author's choice affected your reaction.

To analyze the impact of a specific word choice on meaning, including words with multiple meanings or language that is particularly fresh, engaging, or beautiful, consider the following questions:

- ✓ How does the author's use of fresh, engaging, or beautiful language enhance or change what is being described? How would a specific phrase or sentence sound different or shift in meaning if a synonym were used?
- ✓ How do the rhyme scheme, meter, and other poetic language affect the meaning?
- ✓ How does word choice, including different possible meanings from other countries, help determine meaning?
- ✓ How does Shakespeare use poetic techniques, multiple-meaning words, and language that appeals to emotions to craft a message or idea?
- ✓ How would the text be different if another type of technique or other words were used?

Skill: Language, Style, and Audience

Reread lines 195–225 from *Hamlet* (Scenes from Acts I, II, and III). Then use the Checklist on the previous page to answer the multiple-choice questions below.

YOUR TURN

1. What impact does Hamlet's repeated command to Ophelia to go "to a nunnery" have on the meaning of this scene?

   - A. The repetition shows how much Hamlet now regrets having never given anything to Ophelia.
   - B. The repetition highlights the tense relationship Hamlet and Ophelia have always had.
   - C. The repetition explains that Hamlet no longer finds Ophelia beautiful.
   - D. The repetition reinforces how much Hamlet now distrusts Ophelia.

2. Which statement best explains how the word *fair* is used in this scene?

   - A. The word *fair* refers to Ophelia's lack of beauty and judgement.
   - B. Hamlet uses the word *fair* to link Ophelia's beauty with what he sees as her lack of honesty.
   - C. Hamlet introduces the idea of being "fair" because Ophelia calls his gifts unkind.
   - D. The word *fair* refers to the open and honest relationship Ophelia and Hamlet used to have.

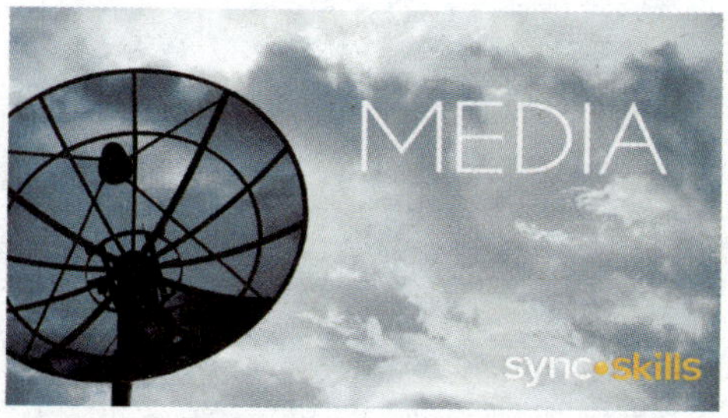

Skill: Media

Use the Checklist to analyze Media in *Hamlet* (Scenes from Acts I, II, and III). Refer to the sample student annotations about Media in the text.

••• CHECKLIST FOR MEDIA

Before analyzing multiple interpretations of a story, drama, or poem, note the following:

- ✓ similarities and differences in different media, such as the live production of a play or a recorded novel or poetry
- ✓ the different time periods and cultures in which the source material and interpretations were produced

To analyze multiple interpretations of a story, drama, or poem, evaluating how each version interprets the source text, consider the following questions:

- ✓ How does each version interpret the source text? What are the main similarities and differences between the two (or more) versions?
- ✓ In what ways does the medium affect the interpretations of the source text?
- ✓ If each version is from a different time period and/or culture, what does each version reveal about the time period and culture in which it was written?
- ✓ Does information about the time period and culture allow you to make any inferences about the author's objectives or intentions?

Skill: Media

Reread lines 169–186 from *Hamlet* (Scenes from Acts I, II, and III). Then use the Checklist on the previous page to answer the multiple-choice questions below.

YOUR TURN

1. How does Sonnet Man explain the idea of having "To grunt and sweat under a weary life" (line 181)?

   - A. Sonnet Man says the line out loud, which helps the listener and viewer know what he means by "a weary life."
   - B. Sonnet Man's version shows people fighting to help the listener and viewer see the experiences of someone with "a weary life."
   - C. Sonnet Man's version uses voice-over with photographs on the screen to help the listener and viewer understand the line.
   - D. Sonnet Man translates the line into his own words to help the listener and viewer understand what he means.

2. Which statement best explains how Sonnet Man interprets Shakespeare's text?

   - A. Sonnet Man breaks down the idea of Hamlet's having an internal discussion by including the presence of others on the screen.
   - B. Sonnet Man's version translates the original words into words more commonly used and understood today.
   - C. Sonnet Man's version removes the explicit reference to suicide that was in the original.
   - D. Sonnet Man focuses less on Hamlet and more on the other characters in the play.

Close Read

Reread *Hamlet* (Scenes from Acts I, II, and III). As you reread, complete the Skills Focus questions below. Then use your answers and annotations from the questions to help you complete the Write activity.

SKILLS FOCUS

1. Identify an important stage direction in Act III, scene iii, of the play. Explain how this stage direction works together with the dialogue to develop the character of Hamlet.

2. Read lines 312–316 in Act III, scene iii. Knowing that *limed* refers to a bird trapped with a lime-based paste, what do you think Shakespeare suggests, denotatively and connotatively, by using the phrase "limed soul" in line 313?

3. Read lines 75–79 of Act I, scene ii, and explain how the overall meaning of Hamlet's soliloquy is affected by the word choice and tone of these lines.

4. Rewatch the "To be or not to be" speech as interpreted by Laurence Olivier and the Sonnet Man. Explain how Olivier's version is similar to and different from Sonnet Man's version. How do both versions relate to Shakespeare's version? What does each version of the speech reveal about the time period and culture from which it came?

5. Throughout the play, Hamlet is deeply upset by his challenging situation: his father is dead, and he cannot trust anyone around him. Highlight two moments in which you believe Hamlet discusses the complexities of what it means to be a person dealing with tragedy. Explain why you chose these moments, and support your answer with evidence from the text.

WRITE

LITERARY ANALYSIS: A soliloquy is a speech in which a character thinks out loud while alone onstage. Hamlet's three soliloquies in the excerpt offer the reader a window into Hamlet's feelings concerning his father, mother, uncle, and especially himself. How does each soliloquy express Hamlet's conflicted feelings in a unique way? Be sure to use textual evidence to support your analysis.

Rosencrantz and Guildenstern Are Dead

DRAMA

Tom Stoppard

1966

Introduction

In *Rosencrantz and Guildenstern Are Dead,* Czech-born British playwright and screenwriter Tom Stoppard (b. 1937) borrows two courtiers from Shakespeare's *Hamlet* and places them at the center of their very own play. A black comedy full of philosophical questions and clever conundrums, Stoppard's play concentrates on the "minor characters" of literature and life, asking questions about identity and society along the way.

"There is an art to the building up of suspense."

NOTES

excerpt from Act 1

1 *[Two ELIZABETHANS*[1] *are passing time in a place without any visible* ***character.*** *They are well-dressed—hats, cloaks, sticks and all. Each of them has a large leather money bag. GUILDENSTERN's bag is nearly empty. ROSENCRANTZ's bag is nearly full. The reason: they are betting on the toss of a coin, in the following manner. GUILDENSTERN takes a coin out of his bag, spins it and lets it fall. ROSENCRANTZ studies it, announces it as "heads" (as it happens) and puts it into his own bag. Then they repeat the process. They have* ***apparently*** *been doing it for some time.]*

2 *[The run of "heads" is impossible, yet ROSENCRANTZ betrays no surprise at all—he feels none. However he is nice enough to feel a little embarrassed at taking so much money off his friend. Let that be his character note. GUILDENSTERN is well alive to the oddity of it. He is not worried about the money, but he is worried by the* ***implications;*** *aware but not going to panic about it—his character note.]*

3 *[GUILDENSTERN sits. ROSENCRANTZ stands (he does the moving, retrieving coins). GUILDENSTERN spins. ROSENCRANTZ studies coin.]*

4 ROSENCRANTZ: Heads.
5 [He picks it up and puts it in his money bag. The **process** is repeated.]
6 Heads.
7 *[Again]*
8 Heads.
9 *[Again]*
10 Heads.
11 *[Again]*
12 Heads.

13 GUILDENSTERN *[flipping a coin]:* There is an art to the building up of suspense.

1. **Elizabethans** people, especially writers, of the time of Queen Elizabeth I

NOTES

14 ROSENCRANTZ: Heads.

15 GUILDENSTERN *[flipping another]*: Though it can be done by luck alone.

16 ROSENCRANTZ: Heads.

17 GUILDENSTERN: If that's the word I'm after.

18 ROSENCRANTZ *[raises his head at GUILDENSTERN]*: Seventy-six love.

19 *[GUILDENSTERN gets up but has nowhere to go. He spins another coin over his shoulder without looking at it, his attention being directed at his environment or lack of it.]*

20 Heads.

21 GUILDENSTERN: A weaker man might be moved to re-examine his faith, if in nothing else at least in the law of probability. *[He slips a coin over his shoulder as he goes to look upstage.]*

22 ROSENCRANTZ: Heads.

23 *[GUILDENSTERN, examining the* ***confines*** *of the stage, flips over two more coins, as he does so, one by one of course. ROSENCRANTZ announces each of them as "heads."]*

. . .

24 ROSENCRANTZ: Heads.

25 *[Repeat.]*

26 Heads. *[He looks up at GUILDENSTERN—embarrassed laugh.]* Getting a bit of a bore, isn't it?

27 GUILDENSTERN: *[Coldly]* A bore?

28 ROSENCRANTZ: Well . . .

29 GUILDENSTERN: What about the suspense?

30 ROSENCRANTZ *[Innocently]*: What suspense?

31 *[Small pause]*

NOTES

32 GUILDENSTERN: It must be the law of diminishing returns. . . . I feel the spell about to be broken. *[Energizing himself somewhat. He takes out a coin, spins it high, catches it, turns it over on to the back of his other hand, studies the coin—and tosses it to ROSENCRANTZ. His energy deflates and he sits.]*

33 Well, it was an even chance . . . if my calculations are correct.

34 ROSENCRANTZ: Eighty-five in a row—beaten the record!

35 GUILDENSTERN: Don't be absurd.

36 ROSENCRANTZ: Easily!

37 GUILDENSTERN *[angry]:* IS that *it*, then? Is that all?

38 ROSENCRANTZ: What?

39 GUILDENSTERN: A new record? Is that as far as you are prepared to go?

40 ROSENCRANTZ: Well . . .

41 GUILDENSTERN: No questions? Not even a pause?

42 ROSENCRANTZ: You spun them yourself.

43 GUILDENSTERN: Not a flicker of a doubt?

44 ROSENCRANTZ *[aggrieved, aggressive]:* Well, I won—didn't I?

45 GUILDENSTERN *[approaches him—quieter]:* And if you'd lost? If they'd come down against you, eighty-five times, one after another, just like that?

46 ROSENCRANTZ *[dumbly]:* Eighty-five in a row? Tails?

47 GUILDENSTERN: Yes! What would you think?

48 ROSENCRANTZ *[doubtfully]:* Well . . . . *[Jocularly.]* Well, I'd have a good look at your coins for a start!

49 GUILDENSTERN *[retiring]:* I'm relieved. At least we can still count on self-interest as a predictable factor. . . . I suppose it's the last to go. Your capacity for trust made me wonder if perhaps . . . you, alone . . . *[He turns on him suddenly, reaches out a hand.]* Touch.

50 *[ROSENCRANTZ clasps his hand. GUILDENSTERN pulls him up to him.]*

NOTES

51 GUILDENSTERN *[More intensely]:* We have been spinning coins together since—*[He releases him almost as violently.]* This is not the first time we have spun coins!

52 ROSENCRANTZ: Oh no—we've been spinning coins for as long as I remember.

53 GUILDENSTERN: How long is that?

54 ROSENCRANTZ: I forget. Mind you—eighty-five times!

55 GUILDENSTERN: Yes?

56 ROSENCRANTZ: It'll take some beating, I imagine.

57 GUILDENSTERN: Is *that* what you imagine? Is that it? No *fear*?

58 ROSENCRANTZ: Fear?

59 GUILDENSTERN *[in fury—flings a coin on the ground]: Fear!* The crack that might flood your brain with light!

60 ROSENCRANTZ: Heads. . . . *[He puts it in his bag.]*

61 *[GUILDENSTERN sits despondently. He takes a coin, spins it, lets it fall between his feet. He looks at it, picks it up, throws it to Ros, who puts it in his bag.]*

62 *[GUILDENSTERN takes another coin, spins it, catches it, turns it over onto his other hand, looks at it, and throws it to Ros, who puts it in his bag.]*

63 *[GUILDENSTERN takes a third coin, spins it, catches it in his right hand, turns it over onto his left wrist, lobs it in the air, catches it with his left hand, raises his left leg, throws the coin up under it, catches it and turns it over on the top of his head, where it sits. ROSENCRANTZ comes, looks at it, puts it in his bag.]*

64 ROSENCRANTZ: I'm afraid—

65 GUILDENSTERN: So am I.

66 ROSENCRANTZ: I'm afraid it isn't your day.

67 GUILDENSTERN: I'm afraid it is.

68 *[Small pause.]*

NOTES

69 ROSENCRANTZ: Eighty-nine.

70 GUILDENSTERN: It must be indicative of something, besides the redistribution of wealth. *[He muses.]* List of possible explanations. One: I'm willing it. Inside where nothing shows, I am the essence of a man spinning double-headed coins, and betting against himself in private atonement for an unremembered past. *[He spins a coin at ROSENCRANTZ.]*

71 ROSENCRANTZ: Heads.

72 GUILDENSTERN: Two: time has stopped dead, and the single experience of one coin being spun once has been repeated ninety times. . . . *[He flips a coin, looks at it, tosses it to ROSENCRANTZ.]* On the whole, doubtful. Three: divine intervention, that is to say, a good turn from above concerning him, cf.[2] children of Israel,[3] or retribution from above concerning me, cf. Lot's wife.[4] Four: a spectacular vindication of the principle that each individual coin spun individually *[he spins one more]* is as likely to come down heads as tails and therefore should cause no surprise each individual time it does. *[It does. He tosses it to ROSENCRANTZ.]*

73 ROSENCRANTZ: I've never known anything like it!

74 GUILDENSTERN: And a syllogism: One, he has never known anything like it. Two, he has never known anything to write home about. Three, it is nothing to write home about. . . . Home . . . What's the first thing you remember?

75 ROSENCRANTZ: Oh, let's see . . . The first thing that comes into my head, you mean?

76 GUILDENSTERN: No—the first thing you remember.

77 ROSENCRANTZ: Ah. *[Pause.]* No, it's no good, it's gone. It was a long time ago.

78 GUILDENSTERN *[Patient but edged]:* You don't get my meaning. What is the first thing after all the things you've forgotten?

79 ROSENCRANTZ: Oh. I see. *[Pause]* I've forgotten the question.

80 GUILDENSTERN: How long have you suffered from a bad memory?

---

2. **cf.** an abbreviation, short for the Latin words for *compare*, used in writing to refer the reader to other material to make a comparison with the topic being discussed
3. **children of Israel** the Jewish people
4. **Lot's wife** a figure mentioned in the Bible who becomes a pillar of salt after she looks back at Sodom, a city destroyed by God because of its supposed wickedness

NOTES

81 ROSENCRANTZ: I can't remember.

82 GUILDENSTERN: *[Paces]* Are you happy?

83 ROSENCRANTZ: What?

84 GUILDENSTERN: Content? At ease?

85 ROSENCRANTZ: I suppose so.

86 GUILDENSTERN: What are you going to do now?

87 ROSENCRANTZ: I don't know. What do you want to do?

88 GUILDENSTERN: I have no desires. None. *[He stops pacing dead.]* There was a messenger . . . that's right. We were sent for.[5]

Excerpted from *Rosencrantz and Guildenstern Are Dead* by Tom Stoppard, published by Grove Press.

WRITE

PERSONAL RESPONSE: One interpretation of the coin flip game is that it reflects determinism—the idea that there is no free will. What do Rosencrantz's and Guildenstern's different reactions to the game's results say about each man's respective belief or disbelief in determinism? Whose perspective do you most relate to and why? Be sure to use evidence from the text to support your explanation.

5. **We were sent for.** an allusion to the events of *Hamlet*, representing the royal summons of Rosencrantz and Guildenstern.

LITERARY SEMINAR:

The Sonnet

Introduction

The informational text presented here offers an overview of the rich history of the sonnet, from the original Italian version to Shakespeare's and Spenser's later forms. Readers will learn the technical knowledge needed to identify a sonnet in the Petrarchan, Shakespearean, and Spenserian styles, exploring how this short but complex poetic form is a part of a larger literary tradition.

"The word *sonnet* comes from the Italian *sonetto,* meaning 'a little sound or song.'"

NOTES

1 The sonnet, a specialized form of lyric poetry, has been used in many of the most **recognizable** poems throughout history. Most people are familiar with the Shakespearean sonnet, with its strict rhythm and final couplet, but sonnets originated long before William Shakespeare. The word *sonnet* comes from the Italian *sonetto,* meaning "a little sound or song." The sonnet was popularized in Italy in the 1300s, and it spread thereafter.

2 Early sonnets were focused primarily on courtly love, but by the end of the sixteenth century, poets throughout most of Europe were writing sonnets to address such issues as the fleeting nature of love and profound questions of mortality. Though the sonnet did not receive much attention during the eighteenth century, it was repopularized in the nineteenth century by poets of the Romantic era, and it continues to be used as a poetic form among contemporary poets.

Meter and Rhyme Patterns

3 The basis of the sonnet is a set structure, with specific rules about rhythm and rhyme. Traditional sonnets have fourteen lines, each of which is written in *iambic pentameter. Iambic* describes a pattern of an unstressed syllable (marked ˘) followed by a stressed syllable (marked /). *Pentameter* indicates that each line has five metric units, or feet. The rhythm in a line of iambic pentameter is marked in this example from sixteenth-century poet Edmund Spenser's Sonnet 75:

◡ / ◡ / ◡ /◡ / ◡ /
Our love shall live, and later life renew

NOTES

4 Iambic pentameter is one of the most commonly used meters in English poetry and verse dramas, in part because of how well it fits with the rhythm of spoken English. In fact, many of Shakespeare's plays make use of iambic pentameter. The unevenness of the five feet in the line suits natural speech and helps avoid the sing-songy quality of even meters. *Tetrameter* (four feet in a line of poetry), for example, is commonly used in nursery rhymes and songs because of the ability to match the meter in the lyrics to the even beat in a melody.

5 Due to its specific structure, the sonnet requires an economy of language as well as a **deft** and technical writing style. However, the most masterful poets have been able to escape the seeming **rigidity** of the meter through small variations, such as adding syllables or beginning a line on a stressed, rather than an unstressed, syllable. These variations not only create interest but can also be used to emphasize significant words, affecting the interpretation of the poem.

6 Sonnets also have set rhyme schemes **determined** by the final sounds in the lines. To identify the rhyme scheme of a poem, begin with the first line, and assign letters, in alphabetical order, to the sounds at the end of the lines. Lines that end with the same sound should be assigned the same letter. In Elizabethan[1] poet Sir Philip Sidney's Sonnet 39, for example, the rhyme scheme for the first four lines is *abab*. The rhyme scheme generally reflects the larger structure of the poem: in the case of Sidney's Sonnet 39, the first four lines make up the first quatrain, or section, of the poem.

Come sleep! O sleep, the certain knot of peace,	A
The baiting place of wit, the balm of woe,	B
The poor man's wealth, the prisoner's release,	A
The indifferent judge between the high and low	B

7 Iambic pentameter and fourteen rhyming lines define the sonnet; however, poets have **diversified** the form over hundreds of years as they adapted to local languages and styles. While there are many variations on the original Italian form, the most iconic and long-lasting are emblematic of the great poets that popularized the form in their time and place: the Petrarchan (or Italian), the Shakespearean (or English), and the Spenserian.

1. **Elizabethan** relating to at the time of Queen Elizabeth I

NOTES

The Petrarchan, or Italian, Sonnet

Bust of Francesco Petrarch (Italian, *Petrarca*) immortalized in Piazza Collegiata square in Bellinzona, Switzerland

8 The sonnet was originally developed between the thirteenth and fifteenth centuries in Italy and Sicily by renowned poets, including Dante Alighieri, author of the *Divine Comedy,* and the artist Michelangelo. The Italian sonnet is often called the Petrarchan sonnet after Francesco Petrarch (1304–1374), the poet who made the form famous with his book of sonnets, *Il Canzoniere.* Many of Petrarch's sonnets are about **unrequited** love, a common topic for sonnets that follow the form he standardized.

9 In a Petrarchan sonnet, the first eight lines (called an octave) present a problem or situation. The last six lines (called a sestet) provide an answer or resolution to the problem. The switch from problem to resolution is called the turn or *volta*. The octave of a typical Petrarchan sonnet has the rhyme scheme *abbaabba,* and the sestet follows either *cdecde* or *cdcdcd.*

If my life find strength enough to fight
the **grievous** battle of each passing day,
that I may meet your gaze, years from today,
lady, when your eyes have lost their light,
and when your golden curls have turned to white,
and vanished are your wreaths and green array,
and when your youthful hue has fled away,
whose beauty makes me tremble in its sight,

Octave
Problem or situation

perhaps then Love will overcome my fears

Turn

enough that I may let my secret rise
and tell you what I've suffered all these years;
and if no flames be kindled in your eyes,
at least I may be granted for my tears
the comfort of a few belated sighs.

Sestet
Answer or resolution

—Francesco Petrarch, "Sonnet XII," translated by Marion Shore

NOTES

The Shakespearean, or English, Sonnet

10 William Shakespeare (1564–1616) is generally credited with being the master of the sonnet in English, so much so that his name has become synonymous with the form. The Shakespearean, or English, sonnet, though still sharing the basic sonnet structure of fourteen-lined verses in iambic pentameter, deviates from the Petrarchan sonnet in certain, precise ways. Typically, Shakespearean sonnets are divided into three quatrains (groups of four lines, each with its own rhyme scheme) and one concluding couplet (a group of two lines). The rhyme scheme is usually *abab cdcd efef gg.* The English form allows for a more detailed development of the question or problem in the first three quatrains, but it demands a quick summary and solution in the couplet.

11 These differences are not as much the result of Shakespeare's own tinkerings with the form as they are the result of his adapting the form to fit a new language. A few hundred years after Petrarch's time, Shakespeare began a period of writing sonnets. The theaters had been closed due to the plague, so to make money, Shakespeare composed poetry. The most popular poetic form at the time was the sonnet, which had been introduced to England by Sir Thomas Wyatt and Henry Howard, Earl of Surrey, through their translations of Petrarch. These translations required technical modifications to compensate for the linguistic differences between Italian and English, resulting in a sonnet that is much closer to its present Shakespearean form.

12 The Petrarchan sonnet features a highly repetitive rhyme scheme; as the sonnet traveled to England, however, modifications to the rhyme scheme were made because English does not lend itself as easily to rhyme as does Italian. For the modern reader, lines may not always seem to rhyme, but consider that English pronunciation was much different in the 1500 and 1600s. In Shakespeare's day, lines such as "Came there for cure and this by that I prove, / Love's fire heats water, water cools not love," did, in fact, rhyme.

13 In addition to evolving the structure of the Petrarchan sonnet, Shakespearean sonnets also explored new themes and subject matter. Traditionally, Petrarchan sonnets concerned the worship and love of a goddess-like woman. Shakespeare continued this tradition, as noted by Romantic poet William Wordsworth, who wrote that the sonnet was the key with which "Shakespeare unlocked his heart." Shakespeare, however, approached love from a less reverential point of view. Love in Shakespeare's sonnets is often less courtly and more physical and directed toward subjects that have more in common with real-life people than the divine.

Spenserian Sonnet

14 A notable third form of the sonnet is called the Spenserian sonnet, after Edmund Spenser (ca. 1552–1599), an English poet who was a contemporary

NOTES

of Shakespeare's. Along with Sir Philip Sidney, Spenser was critical of the lack of an English literary tradition, which he observed was rich in both Italy and France. Spenser set out to craft a unique and truly English literary tradition himself, part of which was his own version of the sonnet. While Spenser was interested in courtship, he was critical of the obsessive love in Petrarch's sonnets. Instead, Spenser allowed the speaker in his sonnets to be more self-aware and the lover more obtainable, which reflected the value he placed on marriage.

15 While the Spenserian sonnet ultimately is considered a lesser form of the sonnet than the Shakespearean one, it is notable for a few reasons. Like the Shakespearean sonnet, the Spenserian version has three quatrains and a couplet, but it follows the rhyme scheme *abab bcbc cdcd ee*. The interlocking rhyme scheme pushes the sonnet toward the final couplet, in which the writer typically makes a key point or comment. Because of this rhyme scheme, the form of the Spenserian sonnet is generally considered to be the most difficult to write.

The Sonnet's Legacy

16 Many poets have been drawn to the sonnet form because of its technical complexity and long tradition. After the period encompassed by the English Renaissance, poets of the Romantic and Victorian periods, including John Keats, William Wordsworth, and Elizabeth Barrett Browning, each wrote many sonnets and expanded the subject matter to discuss religion, history, politics, and grief. In the twentieth century, notable poets such as Robert Frost, Robert Hayden, and Seamus Heaney all composed poems using the sonnet form. Today, poets like Terrance Hayes and Carol Ann Duffy continue to use this pattern to compose new and original poetry that retains the fourteen-line structure. And one humorist, Erik Didriksen, the author of *Pop Sonnets*, has even used it to rewrite popular songs into the form of Shakespearean sonnets. As this 700-year-old form of poetry has evolved, it has continued to inspire modern writers to craft language in technical feats of rhyme and concision as they engage with complex ideas in just fourteen lines.

Literary Seminar

Read "Literary Seminar: The Sonnet." After you read, complete the Think Questions below.

THINK QUESTIONS

1. What are the technical requirements of writing a sonnet, and what are the differences between the three forms? Explain using details from the text.

2. What prompted the first shift from the original Petrarchan sonnet to the English sonnet? Cite evidence from the text to support your answer.

3. Why are sonnets still considered a relevant form of poetry today? Support your answer with evidence from the text.

4. Use context clues to determine the meaning of ***deft*** as it is used in the text. Write your best definition of *deft* here, using evidence to explain your understanding.

5. The Latin word *divertere* has the meaning of "to turn in separate ways." With this in mind, infer the meaning of ***diversified*** as it is used in the text. Write your best definition here, and then try to think of other words that share its Latin root.

Sonnet 18

POETRY
William Shakespeare
1609

Introduction

William Shakespeare (ca. 1564–1616) is regarded as a literary genius and the father of modern Western literature, famous both for his plays and his poetry. Shakespeare composed more than one hundred fifty sonnets, of which Sonnet 18 is perhaps his most famous. Frequently recited at weddings, the beautifully written verse captures the essence of love's timeless beauty.

"Shall I compare thee to a summer's day?"

NOTES

Shall I compare thee to a summer's day?
Thou art more lovely and more temperate:
Rough winds do shake the darling buds of May,
And summer's **lease** hath all too short a date:
Sometime too hot the eye of heaven shines,
And often is his gold **complexion** dimm'd;
And every fair from fair sometime **declines,**
By chance, or nature's changing course, **untrimm'd;**
But thy eternal summer shall not fade
Nor lose **possession** of that fair thou ow'st;[1]
Nor shall Death brag thou wander'st in his shade,
When in eternal lines to time thou grow'st;
　　So long as men can breathe or eyes can see,
　　So long lives this, and this gives life to thee.

WRITE

LITERARY ANALYSIS: In the traditional sonnet form, the poem contains a *volta*, or a "turn" of thought. Where in Sonnet 18 do you sense such a change? Explain how Shakespeare uses figures of speech and tone to suggest a shift or development in the central theme of the poem. Provide specific evidence from the text to support your response.

1. **ow'st** to own or possess

Sonnet 73

POETRY
William Shakespeare
1609

Introduction

First published in 1609, the sonnets of William Shakespeare (ca. 1564–1616) collectively explore themes of love, time, immortality, and beauty. In Sonnet 73, Shakespeare employs inspired imagery to take readers on a journey through life's final season. Through a series of metaphors, the poem tells of the passage of youth, the waning of love, and the approach of death.

"In me thou see'st the twilight of such day"

NOTES

That time of year thou mayst in me **behold**
When yellow leaves, or none, or few, do hang
Upon those boughs which shake against the cold,
Bare ruin'd choirs, where late the sweet birds sang.
In me thou see'st the twilight of such day
As after sunset fadeth in the west,
Which by and by black night doth take away,
Death's second self, that seals up all in rest.
In me thou see'st the glowing of such fire
That on the ashes of his youth doth lie,
As the death-bed whereon it must **expire**
Consumed with that which it was **nourish'd** by.
    This thou **perceivest,** which makes thy love more strong,
    To love that well which thou must leave ere long.

WRITE

PERSONAL RESPONSE: In Sonnet 73, Shakespeare tells a story of aging, mortality, and love through a series of metaphors. In a personal response essay, reflect on your own ideas about aging, and use a metaphor to express them. Does the idea of getting older make you feel anxious, or do you look forward to it? Compare your views with Shakespeare's, using evidence from the poem.

Sonnet 29

POETRY
William Shakespeare
1609

Introduction

Part of the Fair Youth series of sonnets by poet and playwright William Shakespeare (ca. 1564–1616), Sonnet 29 has been referenced by writers and artists from poet T. S. Eliot to composer and singer Rufus Wainwright. In the sonnet, Shakespeare muses on the transformative power of love.

"For thy sweet love remember'd such wealth brings"

When, in disgrace with **fortune** and men's eyes,
I all alone beweep my outcast state,
And trouble deaf heaven with my bootless cries,
And look upon myself, and curse my fate,
Wishing me like to one more rich in hope,
Featur'd like him, like him with friends possess'd,
Desiring this man's art and that man's **scope,**
With what I most enjoy **contented** least;
Yet in these thoughts myself almost despising,
Haply I think on thee, and then my state,
Like to the lark at break of day arising
From sullen earth, sings hymns at heaven's gate;
  For thy sweet love remember'd such wealth brings
  That then I **scorn** to change my state with kings.

NOTES

Skill: Figurative Language

The speaker says "fortune" has eyes, which is personification. This phrase suggests the speaker hasn't had good fortune.

Heaven is also personified as being "deaf," which suggests that the speaker's prayers are unanswered.

Skill: Figurative Language

The speaker uses the word *like* to begin a simile, comparing himself to a "lark at break of day." The speaker calls the bird's songs hymns, which are songs of praise. Together, this creates a rising mood and happiness for the speaker.

First Read

Read Sonnet 29. After you read, complete the Think Questions below.

THINK QUESTIONS

1. What is the speaker's state of mind at the beginning of the poem? Support your response with evidence from the text.

2. Who is the person referred to as "him" in lines 6 and 7? How do you know? What is the speaker's attitude toward "him"? Support your answer with evidence from the text.

3. Where in the poem does the speaker's mood change? What causes this change? Support your response with evidence from the text.

4. Use context to determine the meaning of the word ***contented*** as it is used in the poem. Write your definition of *contented* here, and tell how you arrived at its meaning.

5. Use context clues to determine the meaning of the word ***scorn*** as it is used in the poem. Write your definition of *scorn* here, along with words or phrases from the text you used to determine its meaning. Then check a dictionary to confirm your understanding.

Skill: Figurative Language

Use the Checklist to analyze Figurative Language in Sonnet 29. Refer to the sample student annotations about Figurative Language in the text.

••• CHECKLIST FOR FIGURATIVE LANGUAGE

To determine the meaning of a figure of speech in context, note the following:

- ✓ words that mean one thing literally and suggest something else
- ✓ similes, metaphors, or personifications
- ✓ figures of speech, including
  - paradoxes, or seemingly contradictory statements that when further investigated or explained proves to be true, such as
    - > a character described as "a wise fool"
    - > a character stating "I must be cruel to be kind"
  - hyperboles, or exaggerated statements not meant to be taken literally, such as
    - > a child saying "I'll be doing this homework until I'm one hundred!"
    - > a claim such as, "I'm so hungry I could eat a horse!"

To interpret a figure of speech in context and analyze its role in the text, consider the following questions:

- ✓ Where is figurative language in the text, and what seems to be the author's purpose for using it?
- ✓ Why does the author use a figure of speech rather than literal language?
- ✓ What impact does exaggeration or hyperbole have on your understanding of the text?
- ✓ Where are examples of paradoxes, and how do they affect the meaning in the text?
- ✓ Which phrases contain a reference that seems contradictory?
- ✓ Where are contradictory words or phrases used to enhance the reader's understanding of the character, object, or idea?
- ✓ How does figurative language develop the message or theme of the literary work?

Skill: Figurative Language

Reread Sonnet 29. Then use the Checklist on the previous page to answer the multiple-choice questions below.

YOUR TURN

1. Which of the following explains the role of the metaphor and hyperbole in the couplet?

   - A. The hyperbole emphasizes the speaker's unhappiness, while the metaphor explains the speaker's love.
   - B. The metaphor balances the hyperbole to keep the speaker grounded in reality.
   - C. The metaphor and hyperbole emphasize the change in the speaker's mood from depressed to ecstatic.
   - D. The metaphor and hyperbole show the hopelessness of the speaker's situation.

2. Which two things does the metaphor in the couplet compare?

   - A. The metaphor compares love to wealth.
   - B. The metaphor compares love to royalty.
   - C. The metaphor compares love to hatred.
   - D. The metaphor compares royalty to wealth.

Close Read

Reread Sonnet 29. As you reread, complete the Skills Focus questions below. Then use your answers and annotations from the questions to help you complete the Write activity.

SKILLS FOCUS

1. Identify two instances where the speaker mentions heaven in a figure of speech. Analyze the role of heaven in the poem.
2. Explain the two figures of speech in the final couplet and how the speaker uses them to sum up the poem.
3. Explain how the tone changes over the course of the poem and how that change affects the meaning of the poem.
4. Describe the effect of the repetition of the word *state* in the first and third quatrains and the final couplet.
5. Explain how Shakespeare uses figures of speech to express the speaker's complex feelings and why this strategy is effective.

WRITE

LITERARY ANALYSIS: Explain how Shakespeare uses figurative language and tone in Sonnet 29 to show the speaker's emotions. What is each element's role, and how do the elements work together? Base your analysis on your understanding of tone and figures of speech. Support your writing with evidence from the text.

A Valediction: Forbidding Mourning

POETRY
John Donne
1633

Introduction

English clergyman John Donne (1572–1631) is considered the foremost leader of metaphysical poetry, a movement known in part for its use of complex and unusual metaphors to meld the sensory and the abstract. Donne was a prolific writer across genres, from sonnets to epigrams, elegies, sermons, and more. "A Valediction: Forbidding Mourning" is a poem that explores the complexity of love and connection. Originally written in 1611 or 1612, the poem was published after Donne's death as part of the collection *Songs and Sonnets*.

"Thy firmness makes my circle just, / And makes me end where I begun."

As virtuous men pass mildly away,
And whisper to their souls to go,
Whilst some of their sad friends do say
The breath goes now, and some say, no;

So let us melt, and make no noise,
No tear floods, nor sigh-tempests move,
'Twere **profanation** of our joys
To tell the **laity** our love.

Moving of th' earth brings harms and fears,
Men reckon what it did and meant;
But trepidation of the spheres,[1]
Though greater far, is innocent.

Dull sublunary lovers' love
(Whose soul is sense) cannot admit
Absence, because it doth remove
Those things which elemented it.

But we by a love so much **refined**
That our selves know not what it is,
Inter-assured of the mind,
Care less, eyes, lips, and hands to miss.

Our two souls therefore, which are one,
Though I must go, endure not yet
A breach, but an **expansion,**
Like gold to airy thinness beat.

NOTES

Skill: Poetic Elements and Structure

This is the first of the poem's nine stanzas. Every other line rhymes. I think this is an example of lyric poetry.

Skill: Poetic Elements and Structure

The rhythm changed. The speaker sounds more casual here. Why might Donne have changed things here?

1. **the spheres** the planets in the solar system

NOTES

If they be two, they are two so
As stiff twin compasses[2] are two;
Thy soul, the fixed foot, makes no show
To move, but doth, if th' other do.

And though it in the center sit,
Yet when the other far doth roam,
It leans and hearkens after it,
And grows erect, as that comes home.

Such wilt thou be to me, who must
Like th' other foot, **obliquely** run.
Thy firmness makes my circle just,
And makes me end where I begun.

2. **compasses** instruments used to draw mathematically perfect circles

First Read

Read "A Valediction: Forbidding Mourning." After you read, complete the Think Questions below.

THINK QUESTIONS

1. "A Valediction: Forbidding Mourning" consists of a series of comparisons. What is the first comparison that appears in lines 1–8? Support your answer with evidence from the text.

2. What is the significance of the metaphor of the compass? Explain, citing evidence from the text.

3. Why might the speaker be concerned about the future of the relationship with the beloved? Support your answer with evidence from the text.

4. Read the following dictionary entry:

   refined
   re•fined /rə'fīnd/

   adjective

   1. with toxins removed
   2. elegant or sophisticated
   3. strengthened over time

   Use context to determine which of these definitions most closely matches the use of ***refined*** in the text. Write the correct definition of *refined* here, and explain why you chose it

5. Remembering that the Middle English suffix *-ly* is used to create adverbs, look for context clues provided in the text to determine the meaning of ***obliquely.*** Write your definition of *obliquely* here, and explain how you found it.

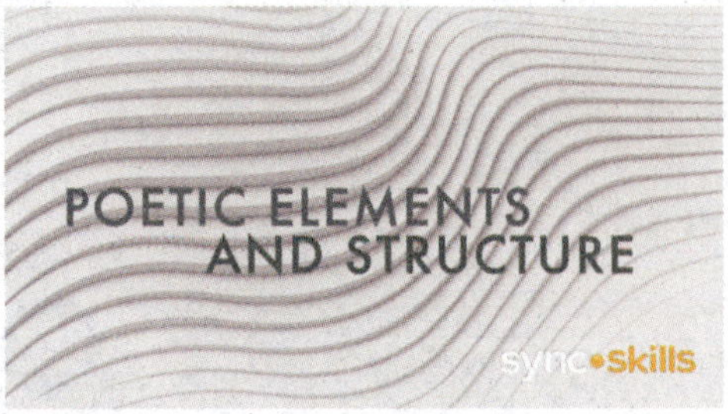

Skill: Poetic Elements and Structure

Use the Checklist to analyze Poetic Elements and Structure in "A Valediction: Forbidding Mourning." Refer to the sample student annotations about Poetic Elements and Structure in the text.

••• CHECKLIST FOR POETIC ELEMENTS AND STRUCTURE

To identify a poet's choices concerning how to structure specific parts of a poem, note the following:

- ✓ the forms and overall structure of the poem
- ✓ the rhyme, rhythm, and meter, if present
- ✓ lines and stanzas in the poem that suggest its meanings and aesthetic impact
- ✓ how the poet began or ended the poem
- ✓ whether the poet provided a comedic or tragic resolution

To analyze how an author's choices concerning how to structure specific parts of a text contribute to its overall structure and meaning as well as its aesthetic impact, consider the following questions:

- ✓ How does the poet structure the poem? How does the poet structure specific parts?
- ✓ How do the poet's choices contribute to the poem's overall structure and meaning as well as its aesthetic impact?

Skill: Poetic Elements and Structure

Reread lines 21–28 from "A Valediction: Forbidding Mourning." Then use the Checklist on the previous page to answer the multiple-choice questions below.

YOUR TURN

1. This question has two parts. First, answer Part A. Then, answer Part B.

Part A: What is most likely the reason Donne deviates from iambic tetrameter, the meter used for most of the poem, in the sixth stanza, lines 21–24?

- O A. Because he forgot the meter in this stanza
- O B. To shock the reader
- O C. To downplay the importance of this stanza
- O D. To place extra emphasis on important words

Part B: Which line from the sixth stanza shows the effect described in Part A?

- O A. "A breach, but an expansion"
- O B. "Though I must go, endure not yet"
- O C. "which are one"
- O D. "Like gold to airy thinness beat"

Close Read

Reread "A Valediction: Forbidding Mourning." As you reread, complete the Skills Focus questions below. Then use your answers and annotations from the questions to help you complete the Write activity.

SKILLS FOCUS

1. In some ways, "A Valediction: Forbidding Mourning" is structured as an argument. Summarize the argument of each stanza.
2. Explain how Donne instills powerful feelings and musical language despite the poem's formal structure and tone. Cite evidence from the text to support your statements.
3. Two themes in "A Valediction: Forbidding Mourning" are separation and spirituality. Use the annotation tool to highlight and explain examples of each.
4. Identify places where Donne's word choice enhances the formal tone of "A Valediction: Forbidding Mourning."
5. One of the themes in "A Valediction: Forbidding Mourning" is the pain of one person's leaving another person. Explain how Donne uses this theme to explore the complexities of being human. Cite evidence from the text to support your statements.

WRITE

LITERARY ANALYSIS: How would the impact of "A Valediction: Forbidding Mourning" be affected if Donne rewrote it with an open form? How would the feeling and tone of the original change, and how would they stay the same? Use your understanding of poetic elements, poetic structure, and figurative language to support your claim with evidence from the text.

To Lucasta, Going to the Wars

POETRY
Richard Lovelace
1649

Introduction

Born into a distinguished military and legal family, the poet Richard Lovelace (1618–1658) embroiled himself in the political affairs of 17th-century England and was twice thrown in prison. Lovelace was among the Cavalier poets, a group of writers who supported King Charles I during the English Civil War by fighting and writing on behalf of the king and his ideals. While incarcerated, Lovelace wrote his most acclaimed poetry, including "To Lucasta, Going to the Wars." Some scholars believe that the "Lucasta" of the poem refers to Lucy Sacherevell, his spouse, who married another man after being wrongly informed that Lovelace had died of wounds in battle.

"Of thy chaste breast and quiet mind / To war and arms I fly."

NOTES

Tell me not, Sweet, I am unkind,
    That from the **nunnery**
Of thy **chaste** breast and quiet mind
    To war and arms I fly.

True, a new **mistress** now I chase,
    The first **foe** in the field;
And with a stronger faith embrace
    A sword, a horse, a shield.

Yet this **inconstancy** is such
    As you too shall adore;
I could not love thee, Dear, so much,
    Loved I not Honor more.

WRITE

CORRESPONDENCE: Using the events and emotions of "To Lucasta, Going to the Wars" as a guide, write a letter to Lucasta from the perspective of the poem's speaker after he has left for the war. Contrast the realities of battle to the speaker's initial claim of what "war and arms" would be like. Conclude the letter with the speaker's hopes for the future of their relationship.

Extended Writing Project and Grammar

Informative Writing Process: Plan

PLAN | DRAFT | REVISE | EDIT AND PUBLISH

As literature from the English Renaissance demonstrates, humans are complex beings, shaped by many facets of life. We each seek to find our life's purpose while grappling with a range of experiences and emotion, which are sometimes exuberant and sometimes painful or difficult. Our goals, shaped by our past, guide us into the future and help us reach our full potential.

WRITING PROMPT

How does our understanding of who we are shape the goals we develop for ourselves?

Reflect on your background, identity, interests, and talents. Think through experiences you have had and obstacles you have faced. Which of these aspects of life have had the greatest impact on who you are now? Select two to four of these aspects. Describe what you learned from them, how you developed as a result of them, and how they affect the goals you are setting for your future self. Your personal essay should include the following:

- a strong thesis statement
- an introduction
- a clear organizational structure
- supporting details
- a conclusion

Introduction to Informative Writing

Informative writing includes a main idea or thesis statement that focuses on a particular aspect of a topic. Informative texts use evidence—such as definitions, quotations, examples, and facts—that clarifies and supports the thesis statement. In personal essays, authors use many of the attributes used in informative writing, but they also use anecdotes and commentary on actual events to support their thesis statement. However, the purpose of informative writing is to inform readers about real people, places, things, and events, so authors of personal essays still need to organize their ideas, concepts, and information in a logical way.

Writers carefully choose an organizational structure, such as definition, classification, compare/contrast, or cause and effect, that best suits their material. Often, informative writing includes visual elements such as headings, graphics, and/or tables to communicate complex ideas or information. The characteristics of informative writing include:

- an introduction with a clear thesis statement
- a clear and logical organizational structure that includes supporting details
- transitions that link sections of text and support the organization of complex ideas
- precise language and a formal or informal style appropriate to the topic
- a conclusion that unifies ideas

Writers also carefully craft their work so that each new element builds on that which precedes it to create a unified whole. In a personal essay, authors often have a more subjective point of view and informal style that readers can easily identify. Effective personal essays combine these informative genre characteristics and craft to engage the reader.

As you continue with this Extended Writing Project, you'll receive more instruction and practice in crafting each of the characteristics of informative writing to create your own personal essay.

Before you get started on your own personal essay, read this personal essay that one student, Monica, wrote in response to the writing prompt. As you read the Model, highlight and annotate the features of informative writing that Monica included in her personal essay.

NOTES

STUDENT MODEL

My So-Called Introverted Life

1 When you look in the mirror, what do you see? I see dark brown hair, hazel eyes, and a somewhat crooked smile. Beneath the surface, though, I see a loyal heart, fierce determination, and an introverted personality. Those are the things that make me Monica, but I haven't always appreciated the qualities that make me *me*. Because I grew up in a loud, gregarious family, I always thought something was wrong with me because I didn't want to spend all my time around other people, especially new people. My family seemed to agree and would shake their heads when I tried to get away from the noise on holidays. During my junior year of high school, however, I learned that being different doesn't mean I'm flawed. Sometimes the qualities that others consider to be your greatest weaknesses turn out to be your greatest strengths.

Background and Identity

2 Schoolwork had always come easy to me. Making new friends has not. My teachers praised my talent for language but always noted that I was uncomfortable working in groups, especially if my best friend wasn't also involved. Kayla and I had been inseparable since elementary school. We were assigned to share a cubby in first grade, and we'd been partners ever since. My family warned me against forming such a close attachment with just one friend. What would happen if the relationship fell apart? I stubbornly refused to seek other companions. My friendship with Kayla always felt like a safety net. With Kayla, I could always be myself. She understood if I needed space and encouraged me to take care of myself. It felt disloyal to look for other friends when Kayla gave me all the support I needed. As we grew older, though, we started growing apart. Although Kayla and I had always been extremely close—our classmates even jokingly referred to us as "Kaylica"—we were also very different. Kayla is friendly and outgoing, while I am more reserved. She loves

NOTES

science and working in the community garden on weekends, but I'd much rather curl up with a good book or write a short story. Last year, Kayla's aptitude in science led her to apply to a STEM program at a local private high school. She was accepted, and while I was thrilled for her, I was overwhelmed by the idea of having to begin a new school year without my best friend by my side.

Interests and Talents

3 The first days of junior year were hard. Although I enjoy being by myself, the school day can feel incredibly long if you have no one else to talk to. Each night, Kayla would call to tell me about the new friends she was making and the new adventures she was having. My heart sank as I realized she was thriving without me. My family's criticism of my introversion and stubborn insistence to remain loyal to a single friend came flooding back. I'd never felt so alone. That's when I made a decision. Like Kayla, I needed to find a new group who shared my interests and who would accept me for who I was.

4 The school's newspaper seemed like a natural fit, so I signed up. I'd thought about joining the paper before but was intimidated by the newsrooms I'd seen on television and in movies. If I couldn't handle Sunday night dinner with my extended family, how was I supposed to work amid the hustle and bustle of such a high-stakes environment? After I dragged myself to my first newspaper meeting, though, I quickly realized how silly I had been. The newspaper office was actually small and unintimidating. Four students sat at computers, silently working on their own assignments. When I walked in, they looked up and offered small smiles before returning their eyes to their screens. These students were all part of the same team, working toward a shared goal, but they were doing so at their own pace and in their own spaces. It was perfect for me.

Self-Acceptance

5 In the following weeks, I began to look forward to newspaper meetings as much as I looked forward to my nightly calls with Kayla. My assignments were tough, especially when I had to interview strangers for a story. Yet my determination to succeed kept me focused, and knowing that I planned to spend time alone to write about each new experience kept me motivated. I also developed strong feelings of loyalty toward the newspaper staff. They might not

NOTES

be my best friends, but they were my new team. With each passing day, it became clearer that I didn't have to change who I was to be happy. My loyalty, determination, and introverted personality might not be the best qualities in every situation, but it turned out that they were the perfect recipe for a reporter. Before I walked into the newspaper office, I had no idea what I wanted to do after graduation, but now I know. I want to study journalism and become a correspondent for a newspaper.

6 Facing the world without Kayla always by my side was scarier than a proud introvert like me would like to admit, but I am grateful that I went through the difficult experience. It showed me that my loyal heart, fierce determination, and introverted personality could be assets for my future. Instead of causing me to be alone and unengaged, my personality can actually help me connect with others because the way I see the world helps me write stories about the world. Now that I know this, when I cross the stage at graduation, I believe I'll have the confidence to pursue a bright future on my own.

WRITE

Writers often take notes about their ideas before they sit down to write. Think about what you've learned so far about organizing informative writing to help you begin prewriting.

- **Purpose:** How do you see yourself? What experiences had the greatest impact on who you are now?
- **Audience:** Who is your audience, and how might your audience connect to your essay? How will you engage your audience?
- **Introduction:** How will you clearly introduce the topic and the main idea of your essay? What language can you use that is both personal and intriguing?
- **Thesis Statement:** How did your experiences affect you? What two to four aspects of life have had the greatest impact on you?
- **Organizational Text Structure:** What strategies will you use to organize your response to the prompt? Will you explain your experiences chronologically or by ideas?
- **Evidence, Examples, and Anecdotes:** What evidence or examples relate to your thesis? What anecdotes exemplify your ideas?
- **Conclusion:** How does the information in the body of your essay relate to your thesis? How can you connect the ideas in your personal essay to your audience or to a larger idea about society?

Response Instructions

Use the questions in the bulleted list to write a one-paragraph summary. Your summary should describe what you will explain in your personal essay.

Don't worry about including all the details now; focus only on the most essential and important elements. You will refer to this short summary as you continue through the steps of the writing process.

Skill: Organizing Informative Writing

••• CHECKLIST FOR ORGANIZING INFORMATIVE WRITING

As you begin to organize your writing for your informative essay, use the following questions as a guide:

- What is a brief summary of my topic?
- How can I organize my ideas so that each new element builds on previous material?
- Can I use visual elements, such as headings, to organize my essay by dividing information into sections?

Here are steps you can use to organize complex ideas, concepts, and information so that each new element builds on that which precedes it to create a unified whole:

- definitions
  > First, define a subject or concept.
  > Second, define the qualities of the subject or concept.
  > Third, provide examples, focusing on showing different aspects of the subject or concept.
- categories
  > First, identify the main idea or topic.
  > Second, divide the main idea or topic into categories, focusing on how you want to explain your ideas.
  > Third, use the categories to provide descriptive details and deepen your reader's understanding.
- comparisons
  > First, identify two texts about similar topics to compare.
  > Second, identify the similarities and differences between the texts.
  > Third, determine how those comparisons reveal larger ideas about the topic of the texts.
- cause and effect
  > First, determine what happened in a text, including the order of events.
  > Second, identify the reasons that something happened.
  > Third, connect what happened and the reasons for it to the main idea or claim.

YOUR TURN

Read the statements in the first column in the chart below. Then in the second column, write the corresponding letter for the organizational structure that would be most appropriate for the purpose and topic of each statement.

Organizational Structure Options	
A	Compare and contrast
B	Advantages and disadvantages
C	Definition or classification
D	Categories and subcategories
E	Cause and effect

Statements	Organizational Structure
Kayla's aptitude in science led her to apply to a STEM program.	
Sometimes the qualities that others consider to be your greatest weaknesses turn out to be your greatest strengths.	
Although Kayla and I have always been extremely close—our classmates even jokingly referred to us as "Kaylica"—we are also very different.	
During my junior year of high school, however, I learned that being different doesn't mean I'm flawed.	
Beneath the surface, though, I see a loyal heart, fierce determination, and an introverted personality. Those are the things that make me Monica, but I haven't always appreciated the qualities that make me *me*.	

YOUR TURN

Complete the chart below by writing key ideas to include in each paragraph of your essay.

Paragraph	Key Idea
Introduction	
Body Paragraph 1	
Body Paragraph 2	
Body Paragraph 3	
Conclusion	

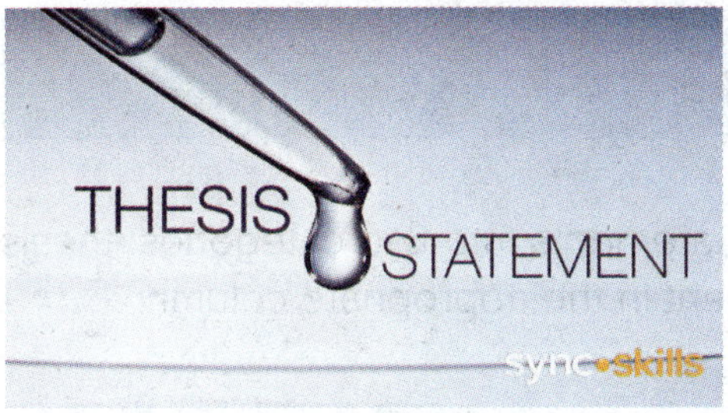

Skill: Thesis Statement

••• CHECKLIST FOR THESIS STATEMENT

Before you begin writing your thesis statement, ask yourself the following questions:

- What is the prompt asking me to write about?
- What claim do I want to make about the topic of this essay?
- Is my claim precise and informative? How is it specific to my topic? How does it inform the reader about my topic?
- Does my thesis statement introduce the body of my essay?
- Where should I place my thesis statement?

Here are some steps for introducing and developing a topic as well as a precise and informative claim:

- Think about your central claim of your essay.
  - > Identify a clear claim you want to introduce, thinking about
    - o how closely your claim is related to your topic and how specific it is to your supporting details.
    - o how your claim includes necessary information to guide the reader through the topic.
- Your thesis statement should
  - > let the reader anticipate the content of your essay.
  - > help you begin your essay in an organized manner.
  - > present your opinion clearly.
  - > respond completely to the writing prompt.
- Consider the best placement for your thesis statement.
  - > If your response is short, you may want to get right to the point and present your thesis statement in the first sentence of the essay.
  - > If your response is longer (as in a formal essay), you can build up to your thesis statement and place it at the end of your introductory paragraph.

YOUR TURN

Read the statements below. Then complete the chart by sorting the statements into two categories: thesis statements and details. Write the corresponding letter for each statement in the appropriate column.

Statement Options	
A	I prefer to keep to myself, but at the same time my friends know that I am loyal.
B	I am someone who prefers to read a book than socialize with a large group of people.
C	Although some people consider my shy personality a weakness, I consider it a strength.
D	It turned out that those qualities are the perfect recipe for a reporter.
E	Sometimes our personalities just need the right context in which to flourish.
F	All my characteristics, both the positive and the negative, are what make me a strong person.

Thesis Statements	Details

WRITE

Use the checklist to draft a thesis statement for your personal essay.

Skill: Supporting Details

••• CHECKLIST FOR SUPPORTING DETAILS

As you look for supporting details to develop your topic, claim, or thesis statement, ask yourself the following questions:

- What is my main idea about this topic?
- What does a reader need to know about the topic to understand the main idea?
- Which details will support my thesis?
- What other kinds of information could I provide?
- Does this information help develop and refine my main idea?
- Does this information relate closely to my thesis or claim?
- Are the supporting details I have included sufficient to support my thesis or claim?

Here are some suggestions for how you can develop your topic:

- Review your thesis or claim.
- Consider what your audience may already know about the topic.
- Note what your audience will need to know to understand the topic.
- Develop your topic thoroughly and accurately, taking into consideration all of its aspects.
- Use different types of supporting details, such as
  - > the most significant and relevant facts that are specific to your topic, make an impact in your discussion, and fully support your thesis or claim.
  - > concrete details that will add descriptive material to your topic.
  - > quotations to directly connect your thesis statement or claim to the text.
  - > examples and other information to deepen the audience's knowledge.

YOUR TURN

Choose the best answer to each question.

The following sentence is from a draft of a student's personal essay on the impact of having parents who speak a different language. Select the supporting detail below that best supports the topic.

> Growing up with parents who speak a language besides English has helped me appreciate the many diverse cultures in our school and community.

- ○ A. Many students at school know only English, and this makes it hard for us to get to know each other because many people in our community speak another language at home.
- ○ B. My parents want me to take Spanish classes at school so I can talk with our neighbors down the street and make friends with their children, who are my age.
- ○ C. At home, my parents speak Polish, and seeing how they have become close friends with the many diverse people in our neighborhood has encouraged me to be open minded.
- ○ D. Do you ever feel like you are the only person who has non-English-speaking parents?

YOUR TURN

Complete the chart below by listing ideas and relevant supporting details that will help your audience understand these ideas in your essay. The first row presents an example.

Ideas	What the Audience Needs to Know	Supporting Details
Speaking two languages also means you connect with two cultures.	My audience needs to understand how speaking two languages helps you better connect with cultures.	Saying *thanks* in English means you are "giving thanks" and acknowledgement to someone. In Portuguese, *obrigado* is the way we say "thank you," but it translates as "I am obligated to you." This is one example of how knowing just one word in each language can help you understand each culture.

Informative Writing Process: Draft

PLAN	DRAFT	REVISE	EDIT AND PUBLISH

You have already made progress toward writing your personal essay. Now it is time to draft your personal essay.

WRITE

Use your plan and other responses in your Binder to draft your essay. You may also have new ideas as you begin drafting. Feel free to explore those new ideas as you have them. You can also ask yourself these questions to ensure that your writing is focused, organized, and detailed:

Draft Checklist:

- ☐ **Purpose and Focus:** Have I made my thesis clear to readers?
- ☐ **Organization:** Does the organizational structure in my essay make sense? Will readers be interested in the way I present information and my commentary? Does my writing flow together naturally, or is it choppy?
- ☐ **Ideas and Details:** Will my readers be able to easily follow and understand my ideas? Have I included only relevant examples?

Before you submit your draft, read it over carefully. You want to be sure that you've responded to all aspects of the prompt.

Here is Monica's personal essay draft. As you read, notice how Monica develops her draft to be focused, organized, and detailed. As she continues to revise and edit her personal essay, she will improve the style of her writing, as well as correct any grammatical mistakes.

NOTES

STUDENT MODEL: FIRST DRAFT

Weaknesses Are Strengths

~~I grew up in a loud family, and I always thought something was wrong with me because I liked being by myself. My family seemed to agree and would shake their heads when I tried to get away from the noise on holidays. During my junior year of high school, however, I learned that being different doesnt mean Im flawed. Parts of my personality used to seem like weaknesses, but later I learned that they were actually my strengths.~~

When you look in the mirror, what do you see? I see dark brown hair, hazel eyes, and a somewhat crooked smile. Beneath the surface, though, I see a loyal heart, fierce determination, and an introverted personality. Those are the things that make me Monica, but I haven't always appreciated the qualities that make me *me*. Since I grew up in a loud, gregarious family, I always thought something was wrong with me because I didn't want to spend all of my time around other people, especially new people. My family seemed to agree and would shake their heads when I tried to get away from the noise on holidays. During my junior year of high school, however, I learned that being different doesn't mean I'm flawed. Sometimes the qualities that others consider to be your greatest weaknesses turn out to be your greatest strengths.

Skill: Introductions

Monica strengthens her introduction by adding a hook. She provides an intriguing question and uses it to describe her appearance and her personality. These changes make her introduction more interesting and better introduce the ideas she will develop in her essay.

Background and Identity

~~Schoolwork has always come easy to me. Making new friends has not. My teachers praised my talent for language but always noted that I am uncomfortable working in groups. Kayla and I have been inseparateable since elementary school. We were assigned to share a cubby in first grade, and weve been partners ever since. My family warned me against forming such a close attachment with just one friend. What would happen if the relationship fell apart? I would not seek other companions. My friend-ship with Kayla always seemed~~

~~very important to me and I did not feel as comfortable with anyone else. With Kayla, I could always be myself. She understood if I needed space and let me take care of myself. It didn't feel right to look for other friends when Kayla gave me all the support I needed. As we grew older, though, started growing apart. Kayla and I have always been extremily close. Our classmates even jokingly referred to us as "Kaylica." We are also very different. Kayla is friendly and outgoing while I am more reserved. Last year, Kaylas aptitude in science led her to aply to a STEM program at a local privat high school. She was accepted. I was thrilled for her. I was scared of the idea of having to begin a new school year without my best friend by my side.~~

Schoolwork has always come easy to me. Making new friends has not. My teachers praised my talent for language but always noted that I am uncomfortable working in groups, especially if my best friend wasn't also involved. Kayla and I have been inseparable since elementary school. We were assigned to share a cubby in first grade, and we've been partners ever since. My family warned me against forming such a close attachment with just one friend. What would happen if the relationship fell apart? I stubbornly refused to seek other companions. My friendship with Kayla always felt like a safety net. With Kayla, I could always be myself. She understood if I needed space and encouraged me to take care of myself. It felt disloyal to look for other friends when Kayla gave me all the support I needed. As we grew older, though, we started growing apart. Although Kayla and I have always been extremely close—our classmates even jokingly referred to us as "Kaylica"—we are also very different. Kayla is friendly and outgoing, while I am more reserved. She loves science and working in the community garden on weekends, but I'd much rather curl up with a good book or write a short story. Last year, Kayla's aptitude in science led her to apply to a STEM program at a local private high school. She was accepted, and while I was thrilled for her, I was overwhelmed by the idea of having to begin a new school year without my best friend by my side.

Interests and Talents

The first days of junior year were hard. Although I enjoy being by myself, the school day can feel incredibley long if you have no one else to talk to. Each night, Kayla would call to tell me about the new

NOTES

Skill: Precise Language

Monica replaces the sentence "My friendship with Kayla always seemed very important to me. . . ." with a simile. She can now better convey the significance of their relationship and the impact Kayla's absence will have on her.

Skill: Transitions

Monica inserts the transition *although* to express the change or contradiction in her relationship with Kayla more clearly. She also adds the transition *while* at the end of the paragraph to better express her conflicting emotions.

NOTES

friends she was making and the new adventures she was having. My heart sank as I realized she was thriving without me. My familys criticism of my shyness and insistentce to remain close to a single freind came flooding back. Never felt so alone. That's when I made a decision. Like Kayla, I needed to find a new group who shared my interests and who would accept me for who I am.

After I dragged myself to my first newspaper meeting, though, I quickly realized how silly I had been. Id thought about joining the paper before but was intimidated by the newsrooms Id seen on television and in movies. If I cant handle Sunday night dinner with my extended family, how was I supposed to work amid the hustle and bustle of such a high-stakes environment? The school's newspaper seemed like a natural fit, though, so I signed up. The newspaper office was actually small. It was also unintimidating. Four students sat at computers. They silently working on their own invidual assignments. When I walked in, they looked up. They offered small smiles. Then returned their eyes to their screens. These students were all part of the same team and they worked toward a shared goal and they were doing so at their own pace and in their own spaces. It was perfict for me.

Self-Acceptance

In the following weeks, I began to look forward to newspaper meetings. I also looked forward to my nightly calls with Kayla. My assignments were tough. I had to inter view strangers. My desire to succeed kept me focused. I spent time alone to write about each new exspereince. They might not be my best friends, but they were my new team. I also developed strong feelings of commitment toward the newspaper staff. With each passing day, it became clearer that I didnt have to change who I am in order to be happy. My desire to be alone and my shy personality might not be the best qualitys in every situation. It turned out that they are the perfect recipe for a reporter. Before I walked into the newspaper office, I had no idea what I wanted to do after graduation. Now I know. I want to study journalism and become a correspondent for a newspaper.

~~My desire to be a good friend and shy personality can be assets for my future. Sometimes the qualities that others consider to be your greatest weaknesses turn out to be your greatest strengths. Now~~

~~that I know this, when I cross the stage at graduation, I believe that I'll have the confidence to pursue a bright future on my own.~~

Facing the world without Kayla always by my side was scarier than a proud introvert like me would like to admit, but I am grateful that I went through the difficult experience. It showed me that my loyal heart, fierce determination, and introverted personality could be assets for my future. Instead of causing me to be alone and unengaged, my personality can actually help me connect with others because the way I see the world helps me write stories about the world. Now that I know this, when I cross the stage at graduation, I believe that I'll have the confidence to pursue a bright future on my own.

NOTES

Skill: Conclusions

Monica strengthens her final paragraph by creating a smoother transition between her body paragraphs and conclusion. She also rephrases her thesis, adding specific details to reinforce the significance of her topic and leave her audience with a memorable idea.

Skill: Introductions

••• CHECKLIST FOR INTRODUCTIONS

Before you write your introduction, ask yourself the following questions:

- What is my claim? In addition:
    - > How can I make it more precise and informative?
    - > Have I included why my claim is significant to discuss? How does this information help the reader understand the topic better?
- How can I introduce my topic? Have I organized complex ideas, concepts, and information so that each new element builds on the previous element and creates a unified whole?
- How will I "hook" my reader's interest? I might
    - > start with an attention-grabbing statement.
    - > begin with an intriguing question.
    - > use descriptive words to set a scene.

Below are two strategies to help you introduce your precise claim and topic clearly in an introduction:

- Peer Discussion
    - > Talk about your topic with a partner, explaining what you already know and your ideas about your topic.
    - > Write notes about the ideas you have discussed and any new questions you may have.
    - > Review your notes, and think about what your claim or controlling idea will be.
    - > Briefly state your precise and informative claim, establishing why it is important.
    - > Write a possible "hook."
- Freewriting
    - > Freewrite for ten minutes about your topic. Don't worry about grammar, punctuation, or having fully formed ideas. The point of freewriting is to discover ideas.
    - > Review your notes, and think about what your claim or controlling idea will be.
    - > Briefly state your precise and informative claim, establishing why it is important.
    - > Write a possible "hook."

YOUR TURN

Choose the best answer to each question about the following introduction from a previous draft of Monica's personal essay.

> Growing up, I was always quiet. I preferred reading books and writing furiously in my notebook over joining neighborhood baseball games and talking loudly at family parties. People would always comment on how quiet I was, and I started to think that something was wrong with me. In high school, though, I found an activity that allowed me to use my quieter skills. Soon I learned that there were other people who thought like me.

1. Which sentence could Monica add to the beginning of the paragraph to help her engage her audience's attention?
   - ○ A. My weakness has always been my quiet personality.
   - ○ B. My personality is very different from the rest of my family's.
   - ○ C. Do you think journalists are loud people or quiet people like me?
   - ○ D. Do you ever feel like you are the only person who thinks the way you do?

2. Identify the best sentence Monica could add to the beginning of the introduction to make it clear to the audience why the claim is significant to discuss.
   - ○ A. I have always struggled to explain and defend my shy personality.
   - ○ B. I am blessed that I am able to work alone.
   - ○ C. Most teenagers have friends who move away.
   - ○ D. Do you ever wonder why you are so different from your brothers and sisters?

WRITE

Use the questions in the checklist to revise the introduction of your personal essay.

Skill: Transitions

CHECKLIST FOR TRANSITIONS

Before you revise your current draft to include transitions, think about

- the key ideas you discuss.
- the major sections of your essay.
- the organizational structure of your essay.
- the relationships between complex ideas and concepts.

Next, reread your current draft, and note places in your essay where

- the organizational structure is not yet apparent.
  > For example, if you are comparing and contrasting two ideas or life experiences, your explanations about how they are similar and different should be clearly stated.
- the relationship between ideas from one paragraph to the next is unclear.
  > For example, when you describe a process in sequential order, you should clarify the order of steps using transitional words like *first, then, next,* and *finally.*
- your ideas are not creating cohesion, or a unified whole.
- your transition and/or syntax is inappropriate.

To revise your draft to include appropriate and varied transitions and syntax to link the major sections of your essay, create cohesion, and clarify the relationships between complex ideas and concepts, use the following questions as a guide:

- What kind of transitions should I use to make the organizational structure clear to readers?
- Are my transitions linking the major sections of my essay?
- Which transitions create cohesion between complex ideas and concepts?
- Are my transitions and syntax varied and appropriate?
- Have my transitions clarified the relationships between complex ideas and concepts?

YOUR TURN

Choose the best answer to each question.

1. Below is a section from a previous draft of Monica's essay. The connection between the ideas is unclear. Which transition should Monica add to the beginning of the third sentence to make her writing more coherent and appropriate for the purpose, topic, context, and audience of her essay?

> (1) I knew I had to attend the newspaper meeting but was scared and really didn't want to go. (2) It wasn't what I thought it would be. (3) When I met the other students, I realized how silly I had been.

- ○ A. Eventually
- ○ B. As a matter of fact
- ○ C. On balance
- ○ D. Another key point

2. Below is a section from a previous draft of Monica's essay. The connection between the ideas in the second and third sentences is unclear. Which transitions should Monica add to the beginning of the second and third sentences to make her writing more coherent?

> (1) It's impossible to predict what will happen in the future. (2) Walking into the newspaper office, I had no idea what I wanted to do after graduation. (3) I want to study journalism and become a correspondent for a newspaper.

- ○ A. Eventually, Prior to
- ○ B. As a matter of fact, Including
- ○ C. Before, Now
- ○ D. Another key point, In the meantime

WRITE

Use the questions in the checklist to revise your use of transitions in a section of your personal essay.

Skill:
Precise Language

••• CHECKLIST FOR PRECISE LANGUAGE

As you consider precise language, domain-specific vocabulary, and techniques related to a complicated subject or topic, use the following questions as a guide:

- What information am I trying to explain to my audience?
- What domain-specific vocabulary is relevant to my topic?
- Have I determined the complexity of the subject matter and whether any words and domain-specific vocabulary need additional explanation?
- How can I use techniques such as metaphors, similes, or analogies to help explain difficult concepts?
- Where can I use more precise vocabulary in my explanation?

Here are some suggestions for using precise language, domain-specific vocabulary, and techniques such as metaphors, similes, and analogies to help make complex topics clear:

- Determine your topic or area of study.
- Determine the complexity of the subject matter and whether any words and domain-specific vocabulary need additional explanation in order to make concepts clear.
- Replace vague, general, or overused words and phrases with more precise, descriptive, and domain-specific language.
- Try to use metaphors, similes, or analogies to make information easier to understand.
  - > An example of an analogy for a scientific concept is *a cell membrane is similar to the bricks that make up the outside of a building.*
  - > A metaphor such as *there is an endless battle between thermodynamics and gravity* can help readers begin to understand the meaning of *thermodynamics.*

YOUR TURN

Choose the best answer to each question.

1. After reviewing the checklist, a student realizes he needs to revise the statement below by using more precise, domain-specific language. Select the best answer that uses domain-specific language to express the ideas in the underlined portion of the sentence.

> I will be the first person to go to college in my family, so my goal is to become a doctor and give back as much as possible to my parents and my community.

- ○ A. I will attend college before any of my siblings have,
- ○ B. Previously, no one in my family has attended school past high school,
- ○ C. I will be a first-generation college graduate,
- ○ D. A diploma post-high school is a dream no one in my family has realized,

2. After reviewing the checklist, a student decides to use a metaphor or simile to explain his idea in the passage below. Select the best revision of the underlined portion of the passage.

> It is thanks to the efforts of my entire neighborhood that I am the person I am today. For some reason, I feel responsible to my community when I complete my college degree.

- ○ A. Like a bird finally leaving the nest for the first time after being taught how to fly by family and friends, I feel responsible to my community
- ○ B. Like the recipient of a gift who wants to write a thank-you note, I feel responsible to my community
- ○ C. I'm a shooting star in the night sky and a rainbow on a cloudy day, so I feel responsible to my community
- ○ D. I feel responsible to my community, which is like an old book that you keep returning to for more lessons,

YOUR TURN

Complete the chart below by revising a sentence or paragraph from your essay draft.

Instruction	Original Sentence/Paragraph	Revised Sentence/Paragraph
Write a precise description of the topic of your essay.		
Revise a sentence or paragraph to include a metaphor, a simile, or an analogy to help explain your topic.		
Revise a sentence or paragraph to include more precise vocabulary related to your topic.		

Skill: Conclusions

••• CHECKLIST FOR CONCLUSIONS

Before you write your conclusion, ask yourself the following questions:

- How can I rephrase the thesis or main idea?
- How can I write my conclusion so that it supports and follows from the information I presented?
- How can I communicate the importance of my topic? What information do I need?

Below are two strategies to help you provide a concluding statement or section that follows from and supports the information or explanation presented:

- Peer Discussion
  > After you have written your introduction and body paragraphs, talk with a partner about what you want readers to remember, writing notes about your discussion.

  > Think about how you can articulate, or express, the significance of your topic in the conclusion.

  > Rephrase your main idea to show the depth of your thinking and support for the information you presented.

  > Write your conclusion.
- Freewriting
  > Freewrite for ten minutes about what you might include in your conclusion. Don't worry about grammar, punctuation, or having fully formed ideas. The point of freewriting is to discover ideas.

  > Think about how you can articulate, or express, the significance of your topic in the conclusion.

  > Rephrase your main idea to show the depth of your thinking and support for the information you presented.

  > Write your conclusion.

YOUR TURN

Choose the best answer to each question.

1. The following conclusion is from a previous draft of Monica's essay. Monica would like to add a sentence that addresses how being an introvert is beneficial, not only to her, but also to people around her. Which sentence could she add after the last sentence to help achieve this goal?

> Albert Einstein was an introvert and look where that got him—the world's most revered physicist! However, there are obstacles too. People don't often discuss the challenges associated with being an introvert. Perhaps we don't talk about it because we are afraid or we think we won't be taken seriously. I am not sure. The gifts that come from such a personality extend beyond me and can positively impact society as a whole.

- ○ A. All challenges also present opportunities for reflection and growth.
- ○ B. Being an introvert has its constraints and takes immense amounts of determination to overcome.
- ○ C. Like Albert Einstein, I have my talents that could benefit the world if they are given the right space to grow and flourish.
- ○ D. I have learned that my introversion and determination allow me to investigate challenging news stories while being sensitive to the people with whom I speak.

2. The following conclusion is from a previous draft of Monica's essay. Monica would like to add a sentence that addresses the part of the writing prompt about goals for the future. Which sentence could she add after the last sentence to help achieve this aim?

> After my time at the newspaper, I started to trust parts of myself that I used to view as weaknesses. Now my heart, determination, and introverted personality help me tell important, true stories. I can finally see that these qualities are some of my greatest strengths.

- ○ A. I wish I could tell my past self that everything would turn out all right.
- ○ B. Even though we have different interests, I know that Kayla and I will still be friends in the future.
- ○ C. As I leave high school, I know that I have the skills to pursue journalism and tell even more stories because now I embrace every part of what makes me *me*.
- ○ D. Although my introverted personality can be a weakness, I know that it is my greatest strength as a friend and as a school newspaper reporter.

WRITE

Use the questions in the checklist to revise the conclusion of your personal essay.

Informative Writing Process: Revise

PLAN | DRAFT | REVISE | EDIT AND PUBLISH

You have written a draft of your personal essay. You have also received input from your peers about how to improve it. Now you are going to revise your draft.

REVISION GUIDE

Examine your draft to find areas both within and between sentences for revision. Use the guide below to help you review:

Review	Revise	Example
	Clarity	
Highlight each example or event. Annotate any places where the connection between the example or event and your main idea is unclear.	Include transition words and explanatory phrases to show how examples and events connect to the main ideas in your essay.	My teachers praise my talent for language but always note that I am uncomfortable working in groups, especially if my best friend isn't also involved. Kayla and I have been inseparateable since elementary school.
	Development	
Identify ideas or events that might need further explanation for your audience to understand.	Make sure you convey your personal experiences using details that help the reader understand what you were thinking and feeling at the time.	Kayla is friendly and outgoing while I am more reserved. She loves science and working in the community garden on weekends, but I'd much rather curl up with a good book or write a short story.

Review	Revise	Example
Organization		
Review your body paragraphs. Are they coherent? Identify and annotate any sentences within and across paragraphs that don't flow in a clear and logical way.	Rewrite the sentences so they appear in a clear and logical order.	The school's newspaper seemed like a natural fit, so I signed up. ~~After I dragged myself to my first newspaper meeting, though, I quickly realized how silly I had been~~. Id thought about joining the paper before but was intimidated by the newsrooms Id seen on television and in movies. If I cant handle Sunday night dinner with my extended family, how was I supposed to work amid the hustle and bustle of such a high-stakes environment? After I dragged myself to my first newspaper meeting, though, I quickly realized how silly I had been. ~~The school's newspaper seemed like a natural fit, though, so I signed up.~~
Style: Word Choice		
Identify repetitive words or imprecise words that do not clearly convey your ideas and experiences to the reader.	Replace weak and repetitive words and phrases with more descriptive ones that better convey your ideas.	I ~~would not~~ stubbornly refused to seek other companions. My friend-ship with Kayla ~~always seemed very important to me and I did not feel as comfortable with anyone else~~ always felt like a safety net. With Kayla, I could always be myself. She understood if I needed space and encouraged ~~let~~ me to take care of myself. It ~~didn't feel right~~ felt disloyal to look for other friends when Kayla gave me all the support I needed.

Review	Revise	Example
	Style: Sentence Fluency	
Read aloud your writing, and listen to the way the text sounds. Does it sound choppy? Or does it flow smoothly? Is the emphasis on important details and events?	Rewrite a key passage, making your sentences longer or shorter to achieve a better flow of writing.	In the following weeks, I began to look forward to newspaper meetings~~.~~ as much as I ~~also~~ looked forward to my nightly calls with Kayla. My assignments were tough~~.~~, especially when I had to inter view strangers for a story. Yet my ~~My desire~~ determination to succeed kept me focused~~.~~, and knowing that I planned to spend ~~I spent~~ time alone to write about each new exspereince kept me motivated.

WRITE

Use the revision guide, as well as your peer reviews, to help you evaluate your personal essay to determine areas you should revise.

Skill: Style

••• CHECKLIST FOR STYLE

First, reread the draft of your personal essay and identify the following:

- slang, colloquialisms, contractions, abbreviations, or a conversational tone
- places where you could use precise language in order to help inform your readers
- the use of the first-person (*I*) or second person (*you*) or third person (*he, she, they*)
- places where you could vary sentence structure and length, emphasizing compound, complex, and compound-complex sentences
  - > For guidance on effective ways of varying syntax, use a reference such as Tufte's *Artful Sentences*.
- incorrect uses of the conventions of standard English for grammar, spelling, capitalization, and punctuation

Establish and maintain a formal style in your essay, using the following questions as a guide:

- Have I used academic language when informing my audience and a personal, conversational tone only when appropriate?
- Did I consistently use the same perspective (for example, using third-person pronouns) throughout my essay?
- Have I used varied sentence lengths and different sentence structures? Did I consider using reference sources, such as Tufte's *Artful Sentences,* to learn about effective ways of varying syntax?
  - > Where should I make some sentences longer by using conjunctions to connect independent clauses, dependent clauses, and phrases?
  - > Where should I make some sentences shorter by separating independent clauses?
- Did I follow the conventions of standard English?

YOUR TURN

Choose the best answer to each question.

1. Below is a sentence from another draft of Monica's essay. How can she rewrite the sentence to eliminate slang and nonacademic language?

> Schoolwork was a breeze, something that I rocked even when I was young, but high-fiving kids in class wasn't my thing.

- A. Schoolwork came easy to me, something that I never bombed even when I was young, but celebrating other students or conversing with them wasn't something I felt comfortable doing.
- B. Schoolwork was a breeze, something that I excelled at even when I was young, but high-fiving kids in class wasn't my thing.
- C. Schoolwork came easy to me, something that I excelled at even when I was young, but celebrating other students or conversing with them wasn't something I felt comfortable doing.
- D. Schoolwork was easy for me, something that I excelled at even when I was young, but getting to chit-chat with kids in class was more difficult.

2. Below is a section of a paragraph from another draft of Monica's essay. Which of the following sentences uses an inconsistent perspective?

> (1) A female student sat at a computer, silently working on her own individual assignment. (2) She was concentrating. (3) When you walk in, she looks up and offers you a small smile before returning her eyes to her screen. (4) She and I were part of the same team. (5) The newspaper office became a place I love.

- A. Sentence 1
- B. Sentence 2
- C. Sentence 3
- D. Sentence 5

WRITE

Use the checklist to revise a paragraph of your personal essay to establish and maintain a style and tone.

Grammar: Sentence Variety

One way to create a more interesting style when writing or editing a draft is to vary the syntax, or structure, of sentences.

English sentences have four basic structures: simple sentences, compound sentences, complex sentences, and compound-complex sentences. When writers use only one type of sentence, readers may disengage from the text. This is especially evident when authors rely heavily on simple sentences. However, with a knowledge of sentence structures, writers can employ a variety of sentences. In the example below, the writer has revised for greater sentence variety and improved the flow of the text.

Edited for Sentence Variety	Not Yet Edited for Sentence Variety
Ronald Reagan was born in Illinois. He graduated from Eureka College in 1932 and worked as an actor for nearly three decades before entering politics in the 1960s. Because he was considered an effective speaker, he was asked to give a speech at the 1964 Republican National Convention. This speech made him more popular and contributed to his being elected Governor of California in 1966.	Ronald Reagan was born in Illinois. He graduated from Eureka College in 1932. He worked as an actor for nearly three decades. He entered politics in the 1960s. He was considered an effective speaker. In 1964, he was asked to give a speech at the Republican National Convention. This speech made him more popular. He was elected Governor of California in 1966.

Notice that the writer applies the strategies of coordination and subordination to combine sentences. The edited second sentence combines information from all three sentences, but it is still easy to read and understand because it includes the word *before* to show that the relationship between the three events in Reagan's life is chronological.

Another particularly helpful strategy for constructing effective sentences is using **parallelism**.

Strategy	Text
Parallel construction is the use of similarly constructed clauses, phrases, or single words. Authors use parallelism to emphasize ideas that are related and equal in importance.	**Black** and **ageless**, he sat rocking **day in** and **day out** in a mindless stupor, lulled by the monotonous squeak-squawk of the chair. Marigolds

YOUR TURN

Choose the best answer to each question.

1. How were these sentences edited for structure?

Sample Sentences: The plane landed. The passengers departed the plane. The passengers entered the terminal. Edited Text: After the plane landed, the passengers departed the plane, and they entered the terminal.

- ○ A. The sample sentences were combined to create a compound sentence.
- ○ B. The sample sentences were combined to create a compound-complex sentence.
- ○ C. The sample sentences were combined to create a complex sentence.
- ○ D. The sample sentences were combined to create one longer simple sentence.

2. How were these sentences edited for sentence variety?

Sample Sentences: The graduating class gave a talent show. Some of the students performed. Other students worked behind the scenes. Edited Text: The graduating class gave a talent show. Some of the students performed, and others worked behind the scenes.

- ○ A. Two of the sample sentences were combined to create a complex sentence.
- ○ B. Two of the sample sentences were combined to create a compound-complex sentence.
- ○ C. Two of the sample sentences were combined to create a simple sentence.
- ○ D. Two of the sample sentences were combined to create a compound sentence.

3. How were these sentences edited for sentence variety?

Sample Sentences: I want to work on the project with Michael. He can work quickly. His work is accurate. He is also effective at making decisions. Edited Text: I want to work on the project with Michael. He can work quickly, accurately, and decisively.

- ○ A. Three sentences were combined to create a compound sentence.
- ○ B. Three sentences were combined into a pair of parallel clauses.
- ○ C. Three sentences were combined to create a series of parallel phrases.
- ○ D. Three sentences were combined to create a series of parallel adverbs.

Grammar: Basic Spelling Rules II

Rule	Text	Explanation
When adding a suffix that begins with a vowel to a word that ends with a silent *e*, usually drop the *e*. When adding a suffix that begins with a consonant to a word that ends with a silent *e*, keep the *e*.	Therefore begrudging neither augury Nor other **divination** that is thine, O save thyself, thy country, and thy king, Save all from this **defilement** of blood shed. Oedipus Rex	*Divination* drops the final silent *e* of *divine* because the suffix starts with a vowel. *Defilement* keeps the silent *e* because the suffix starts with a consonant.
Always keep the original spelling of the word when you add a prefix, even if the prefix causes a double letter.	It is the Nation's resilience, not its rigidity, that Texas sees reflected in the flag—and it is that resilience that we **reassert** today. Texas v. Johnson	The prefix *re-* does not change the spelling of the base word *assert*.
When adding a suffix that begins with *a* or *o* to a word that ends with *ce* or *ge*, usually keep the *e*.	The different accidents of life are not so **changeable** as the feelings of human nature. Frankenstein	The final silent *e* remains after the suffix is added to *change*.
When a word ends in a consonant + *y*, change the *y* to *i* before adding a suffix. Usually, when *i* and *e* appear together in one syllable, the *i* comes before the *e*. However, there are many exceptions to this rule.	The earliest epics date back to a time when most people were illiterate. Recited by poets, probably with musical **accompaniment**, these epics were the **movies** of their day. The Epic and the Epic Hero	The final *y* in *accompany* is changed to *i* when the suffix is added. In *movies*, the *i* comes before the *e*.

YOUR TURN

Choose the best answer to each question.

1. How should this sentence be changed?

> The typical superhero is the personifycation of masculinity, noted for strength, prowess, endurance, and every other virtue except humility.

- ○ A. The typical superhero is the personification of masculinity, noted for strength, prowess, endurance, and every other virtue except humility.
- ○ B. The typical superhero is the personifycation of masculenity, noted for strength, prowess, endurance, and every other virtue except humility.
- ○ C. The typical superhero is the personifycation of masculinity, noted for strength, prowess, endurence, and every other virtue except humility.
- ○ D. No change needs to be made to this sentence.

2. How should this sentence be changed?

> Shakespeare and his peers inhabited an unstable world in which humans were prey to unknown microrganisms that could swiftly terminate their lives.

- ○ A. Shakespeare and his peers inabited an unstable world in which humans were prey to unknown microrganisms that could swiftly terminate their lives.
- ○ B. Shakespeare and his peers inhabited an unstable world in which humans were prey to unnown microrganisms that could swiftly terminate their lives.
- ○ C. Shakespeare and his peers inhabited an unstable world in which humans were prey to unknown microorganisms that could swiftly terminate their lives.
- ○ D. No change needs to be made to this sentence.

3. How should this sentence be changed?

> Browning writes of loving to the depth and breadth and height of the soul, quietly, yet with a passion that replaces past greifs.

- ○ A. Browning writes of loving to the depth and breadth and hieght of the soul, quietly, yet with a passion that replaces past greifs.
- ○ B. Browning writes of loving to the depth and breadth and height of the soul, queitly, yet with a passion that replaces past greifs.
- ○ C. Browning writes of loving to the depth and breadth and height of the soul, quietly, yet with a passion that replaces past griefs.
- ○ D. No change needs to be made to this sentence.

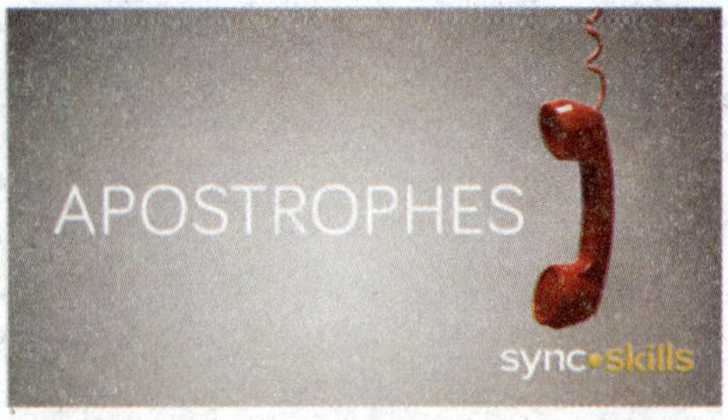

Grammar: Apostrophes

Rule	Text
Use an apostrophe and an *s* to form the possessive of a singular noun.	Is this the custom in King Arthur**'s** house? The Canterbury Tales
Use an apostrophe and an *s* to form the possessive of a plural noun that does not end in *s*. Do not use an apostrophe in a possessive pronoun.	She had been long enough in bondage to other people**'s** pleasure to be considerate of those who depended on **hers**, and in her bitter moods it sometimes struck her that she and her maid were in the same position, except that the latter received her wages more regularly. The House of Mirth
Use an apostrophe alone to form the possessive of a plural noun that ends in *s*.	And so his sons would do after him, and his son**s'** sons, to the final generation. Grendel
Use an apostrophe and an *s* to form the possessive of a singular indefinite pronoun.	"Depending upon one another**'s** hearts, he had still hoped that virtue were not all a dream." Young Goodman Brown
If two or more partners possess something jointly, use the possessive form for the last partner named.	Simon and Garfunkel**'s** list of hit songs is extensive.
If two or more partners possess something individually, put each one's name in the possessive form.	When it comes to tennis, Venus**'s** and Serena**'s** records speak for themselves.
Use an apostrophe to replace letters that have been omitted in a contraction.	The Irish had a hero something like Arthur, Finn MacCool, and stories of Finn spread to Scotland, but that**'s** as far as they went. Conversation with Geoffrey Ashe re: King Arthur

YOUR TURN

Choose the best answer to each question.

1. How should this sentence be changed?

> New Mexico is a state whose history, cultural traditions, and natural beauty deserve to be better known.

- ○ A. New Mexico is a state who's history, cultural traditions, and natural beauty deserve to be better known.
- ○ B. New Mexicos' is a state whose history, cultural traditions, and natural beauty deserve to be better known.
- ○ C. New Mexico's is a state whose history, cultural traditions, and natural beauty deserve to be better known.
- ○ D. No change needs to be made to this sentence.

2. How should this sentence be changed?

> The reputation of Taos as an artists mecca and Georgia O'Keeffes home helps attract visitors.

- ○ A. The reputation of Taos as an artists mecca and Georgia O'Keeffe's home helps attract visitors.
- ○ B. The reputation of Taos as an artist's mecca and Georgia O'Keeffes home helps attract visitors.
- ○ C. The reputation of Taos as an artists' mecca and Georgia O'Keeffe's home helps attract visitors.
- ○ D. No change needs to be made to this sentence.

3. How should this sentence be changed?

> De Niza's and Estevan's one journey did not, however, yield any discoveries of gold or silver.

- ○ A. De Niza and Estevan's one journey did not, however, yield any discoveries of gold or silver.
- ○ B. De Niza and Estevan one journey did not, however, yield any discoveries of gold or silver.
- ○ C. De Niza's and Estevan's one journey did not, however, yield any discoverie's of gold or silver.
- ○ D. No change needs to be made to this sentence.

Informative Writing Process: Edit and Publish

PLAN | DRAFT | REVISE | **EDIT AND PUBLISH**

You have revised your personal essay based on your peer feedback and your own examination.

Now it is time to edit your personal essay. When you revised, you focused on the content of your personal essay. You probably examined how to improve your introduction and conclusion as well as how to make your writing cohesive. When you edit, you focus on the mechanics of your essay, paying close attention to things like grammar and punctuation.

Use the checklist below to guide you as you edit:

☐ Have I used a variety of sentences?

☐ Have I followed basic spelling rules?

☐ Have I used apostrophes correctly throughout the essay?

☐ Do I have any sentence fragments or run-on sentences?

Notice some edits Monica has made:

- Used an apostrophe to make a contraction
- Corrected a spelling error
- Used a variety of sentences

With each passing day, it became clearer that I didn't ~~didnt~~ have to change who I was to be happy. My loyalty, determination, and introverted personality might not be the best qualities ~~qualitys~~ in every situation~~.~~, but it ~~It~~ turned out that they are the perfect recipe for a reporter. Before I walked into the newspaper office, I had no idea what I wanted to do after graduation~~.~~, but now ~~Now~~ I know. I want to study journalism and become a correspondent for a newspaper.

WRITE

Use the questions on the previous page, as well as your peer reviews, to help you evaluate your personal essay to determine areas you need to edit. Then edit your personal essay to correct those errors.

Once you have made all your corrections, you are ready to publish your work. You can distribute your writing to family and friends, hang it on a bulletin board, or post it on your blog. If you publish online, share the link with your family, friends, and classmates.

PHOTO/IMAGE CREDITS:

cover, iStock.com/bgwalker
p. iii, iStock.com/DNY59
p. ix, iStock.com/bgwalker
p. x, Bill Bryson - David Levenson/Contributor/Getty Images Entertainment
p. x, John Donne . Pictorial Press Ltd/Alamy Stock Photo
p. x, T.S. Eliot - George Douglas/Stringer/Picture Post/Getty Images
p. x, Queen Elizabeth I - iStock.com/duncan1890
p. xi, Richard Lovelace- NMUIM/Alamy Stock Photo
p. xi, William Shakespeare - istock.com/MarsBars
p. xi, Tom Stoppard - Allstar Picture Library/Alamy Stock Photo
p. xii, iStock.com/oonal
p. 2, Print Collector/Hulton Archive/Getty Images
p. 3, DeA/Icas94/De Agostini/Getty Images
p. 5, iStock.com/oonal
p. 6, iStock.com/Nneirda
p. 7, Print Collector/Hulton Fine Art Collection/Getty Images
p. 8, iStock.com/Nneirda
p. 9, iStock.com/
p. 10, iStock.com/
p. 11, iStock.com/Nneirda
p. 12, iStock.com/WilliamSherman
p. 14, iStock.com/Massonstock
p. 15, UniversalImagesGroup/Universal Images Group/Getty Images
p. 17, iStock.com/wragg
p. 20, iStock.com/wragg
p. 21, iStock.com/ThomasVogel
p. 22, iStock.com/ThomasVogel
p. 24, iStock.com/Orla
p. 25, iStock.com/Orla
p. 27, iStock.com/eskaylim
p. 28, iStock.com/eskaylim
p. 29, iStock.com/wragg
p. 30, iStock.com/Studio-Annika
p. 31, George Douglas/Picture Post/Getty Images
p. 36, iStock.com/pkfawcett
p. 40, Culture Club/Hulton Archive/Getty Images
p. 48, iStock.com/pkfawcett
p. 49, iStock/Spanishalex
p. 50, iStock/Spanishalex
p. 51, iStock.com/antoni_halim
p. 52, iStock.com/antoni_halim
p. 53, iStock.com/Hohenhaus
p. 54, iStock.com/Hohenhaus
p. 55, iStock.com/pkfawcett
p. 56, iStock.com/Yarygin
p. 63, iStock.com/mizar_21984
p. 66, iStock/Berezko
p. 69, iStock.com/mizar_21984
p. 70, iStock.com/
p. 72, iStock.com/Borut Trdina
p. 74, iStock.com/bodnarchuk
p. 76, iStock.com/bodnarchuk
p. 77, iStock.com/fotogaby
p. 78, iStock.com/fotogaby
p. 79, iStock.com/bodnarchuk
p. 80, iStock.com/
p. 83, iStock.com/
p. 84, iStock.com/Andrey_A
p. 85, iStock.com/Andrey_A
p. 86, iStock.com/
p. 87, iStock.com/gregory21
p. 89, iStock.com/hanibaram, iStock.com/seb_ra, iStock.com/Martin Barraud
p. 90, iStock.com/Martin Barraud
p. 96, iStock.com/
p. 99, iStock.com/gopixa
p. 101, iStock.com/Tevarak
p. 103, iStock.com/Martin Barraud
p. 108, iStock.com/bo1982
p. 110, iStock.com/Jeff_Hu
p. 112, iStock.com/peepo
p. 115, iStock.com/stevedangers
p. 117, iStock.com/Martin Barraud
p. 120, iStock/Fodor90
p. 122, iStock.com/mooltfilm
p. 124, iStock.com/efks
p. 126, iStock.com/BrianAJackson
p. 128, iStock.com/Martin Barraud

studysync

Text Fulfillment Through StudySync

If you are interested in specific titles, please fill out the form below and we will check availability through our partners.

ORDER DETAILS

Date:

TITLE	AUTHOR	Paperback/ Hardcover	Specific Edition *If Applicable*	Quantity

SHIPPING INFORMATION

Contact:

Title:

School/District:

Address Line 1:

Address Line 2:

Zip or Postal Code:

Phone:

Mobile:

Email:

BILLING INFORMATION

☐ *SAME AS SHIPPING*

Contact:

Title:

School/District:

Address Line 1:

Address Line 2:

Zip or Postal Code:

Phone:

Mobile:

Email:

PAYMENT INFORMATION

☐ CREDIT CARD

Name on Card:

Card Number: Expiration Date: Security Code:

☐ PO

Purchase Order Number:

StudySync Text Fulfillment, BookheadEd Learning, LLC
610 Daniel Young Drive | Sonoma, CA 95476